# DEVELOPING TEACHER LEADERS
# IN SPECIAL EDUCATION

Practical and forward-thinking, *Developing Teacher Leaders in Special Education* is the administrator's essential guide to growing special educator leadership in any school, district, or program. Special educators need to be flexible, proactive, and collaborative – qualities that make them uniquely suited to roles in school leadership – but these skills are often overlooked when choosing effective teacher leaders. Featuring helpful tips and detailed examples to demonstrate the concepts in action, this book breaks down the qualities that special educators can bring to your school leadership team and explores how you can leverage those skills to create a more inclusive and successful community.

**Daniel M. Maggin** is Associate Professor at the University of Illinois at Chicago, USA.

**Marie Tejero Hughes** is Professor of Special Education at the University of Illinois at Chicago, USA.

# ALSO AVAILABLE FROM ROUTLEDGE
# EYE ON EDUCATION
(www.routledge.com/k-12)

# DEVELOPING TEACHER LEADERS IN SPECIAL EDUCATION

## An Administrator's Guide to Building Inclusive Schools

*Edited by Daniel M. Maggin*
*and Marie Tejero Hughes*

Routledge
Taylor & Francis Group

NEW YORK AND LONDON

First published 2021
by Routledge
52 Vanderbilt Avenue, New York, NY 10017

and by Routledge
2 Park Square, Milton Park, Abingdon, Oxon, OX14 4RN

*Routledge is an imprint of the Taylor & Francis Group, an informa business*

*Library of Congress Cataloging-in-Publication Data*
Names: Maggin, Daniel Montagne, editor. | Tejero Hughes, Marie, 1965-editor.
Title: Developing teacher leaders in special education : an administrator's guide to building inclusive schools / edited by Daniel M. Maggin and Marie Tejero Hughes.
Description: New York, NY : Routledge, 2020. | Series: Routledge eye on education. | Includes bibliographical references and index. | Summary: -- Provided by publisher.
Identifiers: LCCN 2020011194 (print) | LCCN 2020011195 (ebook) | ISBN 9780367406912 (hardback) | ISBN 9780367415105 (paperback) | ISBN 9780367814939 (ebook)
Subjects: LCSH: Special education--United States--Administration. | Special education teachers--In-service training--United States. | Special education teachers--Professional relationships--United States. | Teacher-administrator relationships--United States. | Inclusive education--United States. | Educational leadership--United States.
Classification: LCC LC3981 .D48 2020 (print) | LCC LC3981 (ebook) | DDC 371.90973--dc23
LC record available at https://lccn.loc.gov/2020011194
LC ebook record available at https://lccn.loc.gov/2020011195

ISBN: 978-0-367-40691-2 (hbk)
ISBN: 978-0-367-41510-5 (pbk)
ISBN: 978-0-367-81493-9 (ebk)

Typeset in Minion Pro
by Cenveo® Publisher Services

# CONTENTS

# FIGURES AND TABLES

## Figures

# Tables

# AUTHOR BIOS

**Courtney Lynn Barcus,** EdS, is a former Instructional Coach and Special Education Teacher in both Chicago and St. Louis Public Schools. She has 15 years of experience supporting teachers, schools, and districts across the Chicago area to implement effective instructional practices. Her research focus is on supporting special education teachers' knowledge development for teaching mathematics. She is currently a special education adjunct instructor and doctoral student at the University of Illinois at Chicago and is the coordinator for the Special Education Leaders for Urban Centers of Tomorrow (SELECT) leadership project.

**Gina Braun,** PhD, is an Assistant Professor of Special Education at Rockford University in Rockford, Illinois. She teaches a wide range of special education courses, and her research focus is on supporting early-career teachers' instructional practices for enhancing reading comprehension skills to students with autism spectrum disorder. Previously, she was an instructional coach for novice special educators as well as a special education teacher for Chicago Public Schools.

**Christerralyn Brown,** MEd, is a former MTSS Coordinator and Case Manager for Chicago Public Schools. Her scholarship interest is in providing professional development and coaching for educators regarding classroom management and culturally sustaining practices to impact student engagement. She is a special education doctoral candidate at the University of Illinois at Chicago with a research focus on culturally adapting social-emotional and behavior interventions and strategies for students of color.

**Catrina Dorsey,** MEd, is a Special Education Coordinator in a large school district and has worked in the field of education for 25 years in both general and special education. She is also a Doctoral Student in special education at the University of Illinois at Chicago. Her research focuses on issues of disproportionality and parent engagement for culturally and linguistically diverse students. Her youngest child was born with special needs and ignited the spark of advocacy that inspired the desire to become an educator and researcher.

**James Hanley,** MEd, works as a Program Supervisor of the Special Services Department for Kirby School District 140 in Tinley Park, Illinois. He has been part of several leadership teams and committees including the Tech Committee, Behavior Team, and the Instructional Leadership Team to name a few. Previously, he worked as a special education teacher for 7 years in both Kirby School District and Chicago Public Schools.

**Laura Kiel,** MEd, is employed as an eighth-grade Special Education Teacher who provides resource services and co-taught instruction in English and Math in a suburb of Chicago. Previously, she taught in an alternative placement for fifth- to eighth-grade students identified with emotional disabilities. Additionally, she serves on school leadership teams to advance the school's improvement plan and to develop a continuum of services designed with evidence-based interventions for students with disabilities. She is currently a doctoral student at University of Illinois at Chicago.

**Skip Kumm,** PhD, is a Postdoctoral Fellow in the Department of Special Education and Multiple Abilities at the University of Alabama. He teaches courses on collaboration in special education and transition courses for youth in alternative education settings. His research focuses on behavioral, social-emotional, and mental health interventions for students with the most severe and persistent needs. Additionally, he researches strategies for schoolwide teams to use a data-based decision-making framework to improve academic and behavioral outcomes for students with emotional and behavioral disorders.

**Daniel M. Maggin,** PhD, is an Associate Professor of Special Education at the University of Illinois at Chicago. He teaches graduate courses in behavioral interventions and supports with a specific focus on students with intensive emotional and behavioral disorders. He leads a number of projects focused on the development of teacher leadership and assisting special educators implement data-based decision-making strategies to support students with special needs. His area of expertise focuses on teacher preparation, evidence-based classroom and behavioral management strategies, and supporting the implementation of effective behavioral supports in schools and classroom.

**Krista McGrath,** MEd, is a Special Education Teacher in Chicago Public Schools. She has taught for 10 years, with both general education and special education experience. She specializes in creating inclusive classroom environments for students with learning differences. She also leads a behavioral health team at her school and has an interest in improving the lives of students, and their families, with adversities beyond just academic.

**Bryan Moles,** MEd, is currently a city-wide Teacher of blind students/certified orientation and mobility specialist for Chicago Public Schools, providing services to a wide range of students in an urban district. He is also a doctoral student in special education at the University of Illinois at Chicago. His research is centered around using three-dimensional printed tactile maps to promote durable cognitive maps and support the development of survey knowledge of an area for travelers who are blind and visually impaired.

**Amanda Passmore,** MEd, has experience as an Instructional Coach for special education teachers, providing in-person support to build educator's capacity in behavior-management, lesson planning, and instruction. She has also been a special and general education teacher. She is currently a special education doctoral student at the University of Illinois at Chicago and a coordinator for the Preparing Leaders in Urban Special Education (PLUS) personal preparation project. Her research interests include social-emotional learning supports through play to support the needs of students with disabilities within inclusive early childhood settings.

**Kasandra Posey,** MEd, is the Director of Student Services for Civitas Education Partners and was previously a Special Education District Representative for Chicago Public Schools. She has over 10 years of experience in the special education field working with a variety of students across in urban school districts. She is also a special education doctoral student at the University of Illinois at Chicago and a coordinator for the Preparing Urban Leaders in Secondary Special Education (PULSSE) personnel preparation project. Her research focus is in restructuring the system of transition services and supports though interagency collaboration.

**Cristina Salvador,** MEd, is a Special Education Teacher in Chicago Public Schools. Her interests include curriculum adaptation, urban education, distributive leadership, and transition. She operates as her school's department chairperson for diverse learners, as well as a member of the postsecondary leadership team, and a mentor teacher. She has earned graduate degrees in both special education and urban education. In addition, she has an advance special education certification in curriculum adaptation.

**Marie Tejero Hughes** is a Professor of Special Education at the University of Illinois at Chicago. She teaches graduate courses in literacy, which are designed to assist teachers working in urban communities meet the needs of students struggling with literacy across the curriculum and directs several projects designed to enhance the leadership skills of educators in the field of special education. Her areas of expertise include teacher education, comprehension instruction for students with learning disabilities and students struggling with reading comprehension, literacy instruction for culturally and linguistically diverse students, and Latinx family engagement in education.

**Geraldo Tobon,** MEd, is a bilingual Special Education Teacher in Chicago Public Schools and is active in the creation and implementation of MTSS systems and procedures and parent engagement around math. He is also a special education doctoral student at the University of Illinois at Chicago. His research focus is in the area of mathematics education for students who are emergent bilinguals with learning disabilities. He seeks to understand the experiences of these students better, how they think mathematically, and how to best support their mathematical development in an inclusive setting.

**Samantha Walte,** PhD, is an Assistant Professor of Special Education at the University of Louisville. She teaches undergraduate and graduate courses designed to prepare teachers to be leaders in their communities and advocates for students with moderate and severe disabilities. She is currently researching and developing tools to prepare teachers to be effective managers of the paraprofessionals who support their classrooms and students. Previously, she was a teacher of students with low-incidence disabilities in the suburbs of Chicago.

**Kary Zarate,** MEd, taught in the Chicago Public Schools for 7 years and chaired her school's instructional leadership team. Prior to being a special education teacher, she worked as a paraeducator and as a wellness assistant to individuals with disabilities. She is currently a special education doctoral student at the University of Illinois at Chicago and an adjunct instructor at Loyola University in Chicago. Her focus is on building paraeducators capacity for working with students with intensive needs.

# PREFACE

## Daniel M. Maggin and Marie Tejero Hughes

The educational context for students with disabilities has undergone substantial change over the past two decades (McLeskey et al., 2012). In the United States (US), the passage of legislation such as the No Child Left Behind Act (NCLB), Individuals with Disabilities Education Act (IDEA), and the Every Student Succeeds Act (ESSA) has codified school accountability as a means for improving the outcomes of all students, including those with disabilities. Coupled with more established requirements to educate students with disabilities in the least restrictive environment, there has been considerable legislative pressure placed on schools and school districts to ensure an effective and appropriate special education experience (McLeskey et al., 2014). Based on student outcome data, however, it is clear that students with disabilities are not receiving the necessary supports and curricular adaptations needed to ensure their academic and social success. For instance, the National Assessment of Education Progress (NAEP, 2019) found that in the US, 73% of fourth-grade students with disabilities and 68% of eighth-graders with disabilities did not meet basic standards for reading with similarly troubling results for mathematics. Given that administrators must focus on the development and implementation of schoolwide systems, and often do not receive significant professional development on issues specific to students with disabilities (Crockett et al., 2012), there is a need for practical resources to support administrators as they develop strategies to include students with disabilities and ensure their academic and behavioral success. As administrators implement these inclusionary strategies, not only will they assist students in special education, but inclusive practices also support the success of general education students who may require similar academic and social supports as students with disabilities.

The prospect of developing systems to support all students and their varied needs can be overwhelming. As such, we advocate for administrators to adopt a distributed leadership approach in which administrators collaborate with members of their faculty on specific tasks, relational activities, and instructional decisions (Talbott et al., 2016). Because special education is a complex, multifaceted endeavor that requires careful attention to issues of compliance, communication with families and community members, and the development of intensive, individualized curriculum, distributed leadership provides an opportunity for administrators to leverage the expertise of special educators to develop effective processes for each of these areas. Therefore, in order for administrators to engage in distributed leadership, it is essential to empower teachers to take on increased responsibilities and contribute to the development of systems (Harris, 2003). It is our perspective that administrators committed to the development of an inclusive school must invest time and effort in cultivating the leadership skills of their special education faculty. Thus, the purpose of this book, *Developing Teacher Leaders in Special Education: An Administrator's Guide to Building Inclusive Schools*, is to provide administrators with practical recommendations for fostering leadership from their special education teachers to assist in the development of effective inclusive schools. The book highlights ways administrators can support and enhance special educators' leadership in their school and leverage their special educators' expertise to the benefit of school overall. The topics are presented in a friendly narrative style that speaks directly to administrators by providing them with research related to the topics, opportunities for reflection of their own schools' context, and strategies and suggestions for implementation in their school.

With this purpose in mind, the following chapters provide administrators an overview of special education with an emphasis on the skills and instructional models that special educators use daily to support students with special needs. We purposefully avoid discussing issues of compliance because, while important, our primary focus is on engaging special educators to contribute to the broader school dialogue around effective academic and behavioral practice to support *all* students. Moreover, it is important to note that the book comes from the perspective of special educators, with each of the authors having experience working as a special education teacher. As such, the book provides an overview of what special educators deem most important for administrators to know about special education and special educators' expertise, in order to engage their faculty in addressing issues of practice.

We conclude the preface with a brief orientation to the book. Each chapter focuses on a topic identified as important for understanding the role of a special educator. We begin with an overview of the professional preparations that special educators receive to highlight the foundational skills and perspectives that ground special education practice. Following the description of special educator preparation, we describe teacher leadership with specific reference to the experiences and activities that special educators engage in daily that make them potentially effective teacher leaders. The next set of chapters discuss specific skillsets that special educators develop through their professional development and practice and include using data, developing and evaluating interventions, and adapting instruction to meet the needs of students with disabilities. The book concludes with two chapters on the special educator role as a school collaborator and advocate. Taken together, the chapters speak directly to administrators on how supporting special educators to become teacher leaders contributes to the development of more inclusive and accepting schools. The book engages the administrators throughout as they are guided to 'Stop and Reflect' about the issues presented and make them consider the circumstances in their own schools. To facilitate the implementation of recommendations presented, each chapter concludes with a checklist of ideas that has administrators assess needs, develop a plan, take action, and monitor progress at their school related to the topic.

In addition, the book provides administers with a wealth of resources they can turn to as they implement these recommendations.

## References

Crockett, J. B., Billingsley, B., & Boscardin, M. L. (Eds.). (2012). *Handbook of leadership and administration for special education*. Routledge.

Harris, A. (2003). Teacher leadership as distributed leadership: Heresy, fantasy or possibility? *School Leadership & Management, 23*(3), 313–324.

McLeskey, J., Landers, E., Williamson, P., & Hoppey, D. (2012). Are we moving toward educating students with disabilities in less restrictive settings? *Journal of Special Education, 46*(3), 131–140. https://doi.org/10.1080/1363243032000112801

McLeskey, J., Waldron, N. L., Spooner, F., & Algozzine, B. (2014). *Handbook of effective inclusive schools*. Routledge.

Talbott, E., Mayrowetz, D., Maggin, D. M., & Tozer, S. E. (2016). A distributed model of special education leadership for individualized education program teams. *Journal of Special Education Leadership, 29*(1), 1–10.

U.S. Department of Education, Institute of Education Sciences, National Center for Education Statistics. (2019). *National assessment of educational progress*. Retrieved January 25, 2019, from www.nationsreportcard.gov.

# 1

# TEACHER PREPARATION

## Skip Kumm, Gina Braun, Christerralyn Brown, and Samantha Walte

Administrators and special education teachers have very different responsibilities and demands throughout the day. An administrator's day is often hectic. It can involve them being pulled in numerous directions, focusing on whole school outcomes, working with schoolwide teams, and interfacing with community stakeholders. Special educators' days are similarly hectic, but typically focus on individual student outcomes, working with IEP teams, and communicating with the parents of the students they serve. However, despite the variability in focus, these two individuals require a similar skill set to be successful at their jobs.

| Administrator's Perspective | Special Educator's Perspective |
| --- | --- |
| My schedule is full for today, but I already know that a few issues have arisen since I left school last night that I will have to address throughout the day. My first meeting is with the schoolwide leadership team to review our state testing results and discuss how we can improve our growth rates for next year. I also have to meet with the community members from our school board to discuss | I have my lesson plans for the day developed and am ready to teach, but one of my students has been struggling lately, and his parents want to meet to discuss his behaviors and academic outcomes. We scheduled an IEP team meeting in the morning to review the student's data and develop plans for interventions to improve his outcomes. The parents also want to discuss his postsecondary transition plan so that he can have a job. At some |

(Continued)

strategies to increase student engagement in the community. Even though my schedule is busy, I also have several observations to squeeze in so that I can provide feedback for my teachers and to help them learn how to address the needs of our students.

point, I also have to observe a few of my students in their classroom to collect data on their academic engagement and to talk to the general education teachers about instructional strategies.

**Key Points:**

- Identify specific **skills special educators possess** that make them ideal candidates to be teacher leaders.
- Understand **why** special educators possess **unique skills and knowledge** that prepare them to be teacher leaders.
- Identify various **strengths** of special education **teacher preparation** that prepares them to improve schoolwide outcomes.
- Determine ways to **utilize the unique skill set** of special educators to improve outcomes for general and special education students.

Administrators strive to provide the highest-quality education possible to all of their students; however, they are increasingly pulled in numerous directions and often have scarce time to focus on the diverse academic, behavioral, and social-emotional needs of their students. Despite their busy schedules, administrators are expected to show student growth, while also meeting the high expectations of the students, families, teachers, and communities they serve. To meet and exceed these expectations, administrators are increasingly relying on distributive leadership models that utilize the strengths of their teachers to lead teams focused on schoolwide outcomes (e.g., behavioral management team, grade/subject teams, and school improvement team). By including their teachers in schoolwide leadership teams, administrators can leverage the collective expertise of their teachers to improve a wide range of outcomes for all of their students.

Both administrators and teachers are increasingly required to provide data that demonstrates their ability to improve student outcomes effectively. To do this on a schoolwide level, administrators work with teacher leaders to develop and implement evidence-based academic and behavioral practices that match the needs of their students and the abilities of their teachers. However, teacher preparation programs primarily focus on preparing teachers to provide academic instruction, and as a result, not all teachers possess the skills required to be effective leaders. For example, effective school leaders are expected to possess advanced instructional knowledge, adaptive expertise, strong collaboration skills, and the ability to use data to improve student outcomes, all while advocating for the needs of the school, teachers, and students that they serve. One set of teachers that receive training on these skills in their teacher preparation programs and utilize those skills daily are special educators. Students with special needs may require a broad range of academic, behavioral, or social-emotional needs, and special educators are prepared to not only meet those diverse needs, but they are also expected to work in a team to collect and objectively analyze data to monitor student progress to select supports and improve student outcomes. As a result, special educators possess a unique skill set that allows them to be effective teacher leaders.

In a typical day, special educators are asked to provide a wide range of interventions (e.g., academic and behavioral) in multiple settings (e.g., general education classrooms, resource rooms, and self-contained classrooms). They are also required to collect student-specific data and to progress monitor their outcomes daily to adapt interventions to meet the specific needs of each of their students. On top of their daily teaching responsibilities, special educators also work as part of Individualized Education Plan (IEP) teams with school social workers, psychologists, speech/language pathologists, physical therapists, and nurses to develop, monitor, and reevaluate IEPs. In this role, the special educator often works as the liaison between the IEP team, the student, and the student's family to ensure the students goals and interventions align with the students' needs, while also ensuring the IEP can be delivered within contextual variables (e.g., staffing and resources) that the school possesses. Furthermore, special educators typically assume informal leadership roles as part of their collaborative experiences working with teachers from across disciplines. The skills required to navigate a typical day as a special educator, mirror the skills required by administrators to execute their jobs effectively.

Students who attend schools with effective leaders are more likely to experience positive academic and behavioral outcomes (Wang & Degol, 2016). To help ensure that all students are in schools with effective leaders, administrators typically receive graduate-level courses and internships on evidence-based leadership practices. However, schools are complex organizations that require administrators to utilize a distributive leadership model that includes teachers in leadership roles. To do this, administrators should utilize the strengths of their teachers, such as instructional or grade-level team leaders, to distribute the workload and promote staff involvement. Special educators are uniquely prepared to assume these leadership roles because they are required to work collaboratively to meet the diverse needs of their special education students. Due to the unique skills that special educators utilize daily, the specialized training they receive in their teacher preparation programs, and the continual training and support from professional organizations (e.g., Council for Exceptional Children [CEC]), special educators possess the skills required to be exceptional leaders.

---

**STOP AND REFLECT**

1. How have the schools that you have worked in utilize special education teachers?
2. In what roles could special education teachers make exceptional leaders?
3. How can administrators provide supports that allow special education teachers to grow as leaders?

---

## Special Education Teacher Preparation

There is undoubtedly a significant link between teacher effectiveness and student achievement (e.g., Darling-Hammond & Ducommun, 2010; Pretorius, 2012). Thus, adequately preparing teachers both in their preservice programs and ongoing in-service support is critical. Determining the essential components necessary to enhance teacher capacity for effective instruction is no easy task due to the complexities of teaching (Shepherd et al., 2016). This is especially true for special educators who often experience common challenges due to role ambiguity and confusion on the best methods for intervention and evaluation (Leko et al., 2015).

### Role Ambiguity

Special educators balance many roles, such as serving as interventionists, coaches, and case managers across varied instructional settings that include general education, resource, and self-contained classrooms. This wide variety of duties often leads to ill-defined responsibilities, making it difficult for special educators to support students to the best of their abilities (Slanda, 2017). Special educators balance their day-to-day teaching responsibilities that include providing instruction in a separate setting as well as collaborating with a co-teacher in an inclusive setting (Billingsley et al., 2004), which require two separate sets of skills, resources, preparation, instruction, and time. Clear expectations and responsibilities in each instructional setting is a critical component for supporting special educator success (Rock et al., 2016). With the implementation of preventive frameworks such as Multi-Tiered Systems of Support (MTSS), there is often confusion as to the role of special educators within the system (Lignugaris et al., 2014). Both general and special educators should be responsible for collecting data and implementing interventions for at-risk students (Brownell et al., 2010). It is recommended for school leaders to develop a systematic framework, such as MTSS, that is run by a leadership team representing all stakeholders, including special educators, who can develop a clear process within the school with well-defined roles for all educators (Freeman et al., 2015).

## Teacher Evaluation

Over the last two decades, discussions of teacher accountability and effectiveness or quality have been a priority as they connect to student achievement. When considering how to ensure teachers meet high expectations in these areas, teacher evaluations have been a recommended and widely implemented solution (Minnici, 2014). As an administrator, conducting evaluations is a primary responsibility, and they should provide more than scores to assess job performance. Evaluations should provide an opportunity for administrators to provide feedback and support to enhance teacher effectiveness. However, there remains confusion on the best methods to evaluate special educators (Holdheide et al., 2010), and in turn, leaves administrators with a lack of clarity on how to provide the best support to special educators. For instance, test scores represent an important part of teacher evaluations. However, teachers of students with special needs often have several factors affecting their scores, including students who work with significantly modified curriculum, make accommodations for testing, or must consider chronic absenteeism of students due to health issues. Thus, there are arguments as to whether or not standardized assessments are an adequate measure of teacher effectiveness, especially for special educators (Rock et al., 2016).

## Preservice Preparation

Despite these challenges, common practices, knowledge, and skills have been researched and recommended as critical components for developing effective special educators. Preparation programs continue to develop as special educators' roles have changed (Leko et al., 2015), and new policies supporting accessible and equitable instruction for all students influence teacher preparation programs (Scheeler et al., 2016). For example, preparation programs include opportunities for preservice teachers to build knowledge in the best inclusive practices such as collaboration and co-teaching (Shin et al., 2016). Effective special educators have a breadth and depth of pedagogical knowledge, including the development of and methods for an array of academic and behavior skills. Special educators can determine appropriate evidence-based instructional practices, interventions, and assessments, and implement them with fidelity. They also possess the skills to differentiate and individualize for diverse learners (Sharp et al., 2019). Special educators are prepared for the utilization of technology in the classroom, including assistive technology, and for ways to consider culturally and linguistically diverse students in their planning and instruction (Rock et al., 2016).

To effectively develop the knowledge and skills needed to be successful in a special education placement, research recommends that several practices be enacted (e.g., Brownell et al., 2010; Rock et al., 2016; Scheeler et al., 2016). Through preparation programs, special educators gain an awareness of effective instructional skills, including the impact of their decisions, their strengths, and areas for growth (Scheeler et al., 2016) becoming reflective practitioners (Whitaker & Valtierra, 2018). Throughout all aspects of their development as a preservice educator, future special educators are provided opportunities to develop content knowledge, effectively instruct students using evidence-based practices (EBPs), and reflect on learning and practice in meaningful ways (Leko et al., 2015). Preparation programs also provide opportunities for preservice educators to engage in meaningful field experiences, applying what they learn in the university classroom (Sharp et al., 2019), so they begin their careers with meaningful and relevant experiences. Research on EBPs continues to emerge, showing that certain strategies have a positive impact on student learning (Scheeler et al., 2016); however, despite an introduction to both the theory and practice of EBPs, as well as opportunities to apply them in preservice preparation programs, research demonstrates that in-service teachers are not confident in, nor implement EBPs with fidelity, specifically in the diverse context of their classrooms. Thus, special educators need increased preparation both during preservice and in-service on how to support the implementation of effective practices (Guckert et al., 2016). Skills that should be supported are selecting, implementing, and evaluating these practices within the context of their classrooms and individual needs of their students.

Preparing special educators is complex because their roles and responsibilities are the same. The critical components that are included in teacher preparation programs provide teachers with a core foundation in knowledge and pedagogy. However, preservice programs are not the end of teacher preparation. Once they become teachers of record, it is the responsibility of the school leadership team to provide adequate support and development of all teachers. When planning to support special educators, especially new or novice teachers, school leaders should consider their preparedness for supporting special educators to promote a schoolwide inclusive environment. To examine their own beliefs and practices, school administrations can use the Innovation Configurations (ICs) for principal leadership: Moving toward inclusive and high-achieving schools for students with disabilities (Billingsley et al., 2019). The components provide administrators with essential practices and considerations for their schools, specifically related to supporting inclusive practices, including the special educators (see Appendix B). It is recommended for administrators to utilize tools such as these to self-evaluate their practice (Scheeler et al., 2016). In doing so, administrators will have more success in supporting special education teachers, especially novice special educators.

---

## STOP AND REFLECT

1. What are the critical skills special education teachers must possess to be effective for their students?
2. As an administrator, what is your role in teacher preparation and continued professional development?

---

## Novice Special Education Induction

The demanding roles of special educators' often lead to teacher burnout (Conley & You, 2017). School leaders need to understand the complexities and demands of a special educator to better to support them. Products of the stress special educators experience include attrition from the field, which contributes to the chronic shortage of special educators across the United States (Hagaman & Casey, 2018). Research documents the varied reasons why special educators leave their jobs; however, the most common tend to be teachers reports of lack of knowledge and preparedness for their role, poor conditions, such as large caseloads and lack of other related supports, lack of respect across the building, and lack of administrative support (Hagaman & Casey, 2018). Special educators must be highly skilled in assessing and analyzing data, determining and implementing effective interventions for students with a wide range of both academic and behavioral needs (Rock et al., 2016), as well as identifying ways to support students' specific needs to provide effective, individualized supports while also giving students access to grade-level curriculum (Vittek, 2015). They must have skills in writing quality IEPs, collaborating with general education teachers, paraprofessionals, families, and other related service providers (Shin et al., 2016). The demands of special educators are often stressful, and thus, lead to teacher burnout. Because of special educator shortages and frequent attrition, highly qualified teachers are often unavailable to provide services and as a result, student achievement is affected. Schools and districts then have the burden of increased financial costs, to recruit new teachers, provide induction training, and professionally develop these individuals, only for the cycle to begin again (Langher et al., 2017). To combat teacher shortages and attrition, school administrators should consider these critical components: induction supports, ongoing professional development, administrative supports, and the implementation of special education teacher leadership (e.g., Vittek, 2015).

## Induction Supports and Professional Development

School administrators are responsible for ensuring their teachers are prepared to teach in their schools, from logistical details to instructional practices; all teachers must be clear of their expectations and have support to be effective educators. Providing all of their new teachers with inductive supports allows new teachers to get acclimated to the school culture and community and grow capacity in classroom management and instruction (Bettini et al., 2017). Mentoring programs are a useful strategy for supporting new special education teachers. Research shows the benefits of providing teachers with access to someone who works with similar populations to provide targeted, practical supports (Vittek, 2015). Aside from mentorship or instructional coaching as a means for professional development, providing opportunities for special education teachers to attend targeted professional developments will increase their knowledge, skills, and confidence, leading to more positive outcomes for students. Likewise, it provides opportunities for teachers to have leadership opportunities by returning to school and presenting on the newly learned information.

Providing meaningful and quality professional development to educators can be daunting. This is especially true for special educators (McLeskey et al., 2017). Because of many of the reasons discussed in this section, including the complexities of the knowledge and skills special educators need and ongoing confusion of their roles and responsibilities, providing the correct professional development and support is challenging and their unique needs must be considered. Special educators report that meaningful and useful professional development is targeted to their specific roles and relevant needs. Also, they appreciate and grow from opportunities to collaborate with other special educators (Jones et al., 2013). Successful professional development includes skills targeted to the specific needs of the teachers, opportunities to practice, and gain feedback (Darling-Hammond et al., 2017). The goal of providing induction programs and professional development helps educators have successful early career experiences. Likewise, it's the first step in administrators providing meaningful supports to their teachers (Vittek, 2015).

## Administrator Support

Research shows that a lack of administrative support can significantly affect educators' attrition rates (Conley & You, 2017). Administrators can show support to their special educators by considering their specific needs when planning for the school culture and climate (Vittek, 2015). For example, when creating a schedule for the entire school, the needs of special education students, including their IEP minutes, must be a priority to ensure all of the students' needs are being met, and special educators can adequately do their jobs. This alleviates scheduling conflicts that many special educators face at the beginning and throughout the school year. Likewise, when planning for the schools' schedule, they should ensure special educators have adequate preparation times and collaborative opportunities with co-teachers and paraprofessionals. A strong school leader will ensure their culture and climate is inclusive of all teachers. This also includes how to consider special educators for leadership positions.

### *Special Educator Leadership*

As special educators develop, it is essential to give them leadership opportunities. Effectively run schools are those in which equal representation across grade level and content are considered, including special education (Spillane et al., 2004). Teachers who are involved in leadership are more likely to stay in their positions, thus leading to less teacher turnover (Reeves & Lowenhaupt, 2016). Often, principals do not have in-depth knowledge and skills in special education; thus, it makes it difficult to adequately do things such as complete evaluations and provide meaningful and relevant support and professional development. However, working alongside special education teacher leaders as collaborators, schoolwide instructional coaches, or intervention specialists will not only support in growing the capacity of administrators, but also fosters a climate of inclusivity.

To adequately prepare and support novice special educators, administrators should ensure their teachers are provided access to resources, collaborative opportunities with colleagues within and outside of the school, targeted professional development, and ongoing support through coaching and in-house mentoring. By providing leadership opportunities, teachers gain motivation to stay in their current positions and continue to develop effective skills because they feel they have a greater sense of purpose and play a critical role in their schoolwide practices and initiatives.

---

**STOP AND REFLECT**

1. What challenges might novice special education teachers face that causes a high level of attrition?
2. As a school administrator, what can you do to ensure the retention of quality special educators?

## Connections to Professional Standards

The CEC (2015) developed rigorous standards for special educators to follow. The CEC Initial Preparation Standards give benchmarks for special educators seeking their initial teaching certification. These seven standards are organized into four areas of focus: learner and learning, content knowledge and professional foundations, instructional pedagogy, and professionalism and collaboration. The underlying theme of the guidelines is that beginning special educators will have a solid knowledge base of effective practices and that they will collaborate with all relevant stakeholders. When certified special educators seek advanced certification (e.g., master's degree in special education), their programs educate them using the CEC Advanced Preparation Standards. As special educators gain more experience in their roles, the expectation is that they will have mastered instruction and tackle additional responsibilities that will improve and advance the field. Collaboration and effective practices are still essential, but advanced performance is now the expectation in the areas of assessment, research and inquiry, and leadership and policy.

Leadership is also emphasized throughout CEC's (2015) Standards for Professional Practice, which applies to all special educators. Specific references to conflict resolution, active participation in planning and evaluation of special education programs, collaboration with a variety of colleagues, and an entire section on the management of para educators are provided (see Appendix B). The CEC standards are advanced as national guidelines to ensure quality in the profession, but many individual state standards include language that addresses students with special needs. Some states, like Illinois, specifically cover multiple areas related to special educators, like assessment, inclusion, and collaboration. Others, however, only discuss differentiation or identification (White et al., 2009). It is important for administrators to familiarize themselves with the CEC standards and to use them in conjunction with their own state's standards to develop an understanding of what to expect from special educators.

---

**STOP AND REFLECT**

After reviewing the professional standards for special educators:

1. What should administrators expect from novice special educators?
2. What should administrators expect from experienced special educators?
3. What knowledge or training do administrators need to support special educators in the areas highlighted by the standards?

## Developing Skills to Promote Special Educator Leadership

Teacher preparation programs can prepare preservice educators to engage in curriculum building, data-based decision-making, and to use research to inform their teaching, thereby developing many of the skills we expect to see in teacher leaders. Teacher leadership is not necessarily about formal roles, but about teachers extending their presence beyond the classroom by seeking additional challenges and growth opportunities (Liston et al., 2008). To help foster leadership development, administrators can offer preservice educators opportunities to leave the isolation of the classroom during student teaching to collaborate with others and build leadership capacity (Dozier, 2007). Mentor teachers can encourage these opportunities for preservice educators to learn how in-service educators contribute to the decision-making process in school communities (Johnson & Donaldson, 2007). Cooperative learning experiences promote learning by teaching, learning by doing, and learning by collaborating, thus increasing the development of leadership skills.

### *Developing and Extending Preservice Skills*

Developing special educator teacher leadership involves engaging in new kinds of decision-making, fostering mentoring skills, knowledge production, peer coaching, and continuous professional development. These skills promoting teacher leadership can be embedded in tasks and roles that do not create artificial, imposed formal hierarchies and positions. The administrator can provide opportunities for leadership available to all teachers without regard to formal roles and titles. Teachers must be prepared to function in schools that are restructured to meet the needs of diverse learners well through collaboration and decision-making.

Collaboration is a skill that gives all teachers the opportunity to have input in the decision-making process (Kohm & Nance, 2009). Subsequently, everyone benefits from the multiple ideas that are shared rather than the ideas of one leader or administrator (Cosenza, 2015). When teachers work cooperatively, they become empowered as leaders, and in the long run, everyone benefits. If teacher leadership is directly linked to teacher learning through collaboration, it is the job of teacher preparation programs to foster this development. During teacher preparation programs, preservice educators should be provided with opportunities to lead and learn continuously as they inquire into more responsive practices.

Another skill that fosters special educator leadership is sharing EBPs as ways to influence others and provide guidance to peers. There is an underlying belief that this is also empowering because the sharing of best practices has a positive impact on the learning of colleagues as well as students. This process is reciprocal in nature in that teachers who share can become enriched in return when others share their best practices with them (Darling-Hammond et al., 2019). Role modeling, another skill that fosters leadership, can be viewed by administrators as an obligation to demonstrate respectful behaviors, professional dispositions, and high-quality character traits. Providing preservice educators with clear roles provides practice to effect change or serve as a representative of their peers in a larger group such as the classroom or leading a planning meeting (Pont et al., 2008). Often, preservice educators believe that schools provide clearly defined roles with attached levels of leadership and influence. They assume that being appointed to these formal roles is an empowering opportunity and overall seem to view leadership as something that is official in nature, requiring a title (Darling-Hammond et al., 1995). During early career teaching, there is an underlying belief that unless teachers have a formal title, they had very little voice in the decision-making process (Mulford, 2003). When educators are given an opportunity to engage in collaboration, decision-making, and mentoring, administrators can shift this perspective early in educators' careers. In turn, engaging novice teachers in the important reciprocal sharing process that is so effective for professional growth.

It is clear that the teachers can be leaders either with or without the support of an administrator and that a collaborative environment is key to both the success of the school and the academic performance of the young students (Mulford, 2003). Increasingly, teachers are beginning to view their roles as much more than delivering a specific curriculum within the confines of a classroom. Special educators increasingly want to use their skills to better outcomes on a schoolwide level. It is critical for administrators to empower leadership before an educator steps foot inside the classroom.

## Summary

Administrators have demanding job responsibilities that require them to address a wide range of academic, behavioral, and supervisory issues on a daily basis. Furthermore, administrators are expected to demonstrate yearly student growth on standardized test scores and numerous other outcome measures. To meet these demands, administrators rely on teachers to contribute to schoolwide initiatives through assuming leadership roles on targeted schoolwide teams (e.g., PBIS [Positive Behavior Intervention Support] team, grade-level teams, and content teams). However, many teachers lack the training or skill set to lead teams that analyze data to guide the delivery of instructional or behavioral frameworks that can meet the diverse needs of all the students and staff in a school. Due to the unique demands of teaching students with special needs and professional standards focused on whole-child initiatives, special educators receive preservice training and experience that provides them with the diverse skills required to be an exceptional schoolwide leader. Administrators who leverage special educator's leadership abilities through a structured induction program, ongoing professional development, and provide administrative support can improve schoolwide outcomes by utilizing a distributed leadership model that allows special educators to utilize their unique strengths and abilities in leadership positions.

## Next Steps

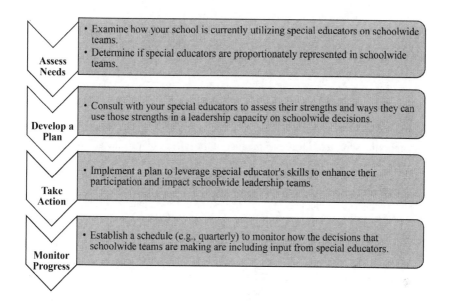

**Assess Needs**
- Examine how your school is currently utilizing special educators on schoolwide teams.
- Determine if special educators are proportionately represented in schoolwide teams.

**Develop a Plan**
- Consult with your special educators to assess their strengths and ways they can use those strengths in a leadership capacity on schoolwide decisions.

**Take Action**
- Implement a plan to leverage special educator's skills to enhance their participation and impact schoolwide leadership teams.

**Monitor Progress**
- Establish a schedule (e.g., quarterly) to monitor how the decisions that schoolwide teams are making are including input from special educators.

## References

Anderson, C. (2014, March). *Bill and Melinda Gates: Why giving away our wealth has been the most satisfying this we've done* [Video]. TED Conferences. https://www.ted.com/talks/bill_and_melinda_gates_why_giving_away_our_wealth_has_been_the_most_satisfying_thing_we_ve_done

Bettini, E., Benedict, A., Thomas, R., Kimerling, J., Choi, N., & McLeskey, J. (2017). Cultivating a community of effective special education teachers: Local special education administrators' roles. *Remedial and Special Education, 38*(2), 111–126. https://doi.org/10.1177/0741932516664790

Billingsley, B., Carlson, E., & Klein, S. (2004). The working conditions and induction support of early career special educators. *Exceptional Children, 70*(3), 333–347. https://doi.org/10.1177/001440290407000305

Billingsley, B., McLeskey, J., & Crockett, J.B. (2019). Conceptualizing principal leadership for effective inclusive schools. In J. B. Crockett, B. Billingsley, & M. L. Boscardin (Eds.), *Handbook of leadership and administration for special education* (2nd ed., pp. 306–332). Routledge. https://doi.org/10.4324/9781315226378-19

Brownell, M.T., Sindelar, P.T., Kiely, M.T., & Danielson, L.C. (2010). Special education teacher quality and preparation: Exposing foundations, constructing a new model. *Exceptional Children, 76*(3), 357–377. https://doi.org/10.1177/001440291007600307

Conley, S., & You, S. (2017). Key influences on special education teachers' intentions to leave: The effects of administrative support and teacher team efficacy in a mediational model. *Educational Management Administration & Leadership, 45*(3), 521–540. https://doi.org/10.1177/1741143215608859

Cosenza, M.N. (2015). Defining teacher leadership: Affirming the teacher leader model standards. *Issues in Teacher Education, 24*(2), 79–99.

Council for Exceptional Children (CEC). (2015). *What every special educator must know: Professional ethics and standards* (7th ed.). Council for Exceptional Children.

Darling-Hammond, L., Bullmaster, M.L., & Cobb, V.L. (1995). Rethinking teacher leadership through professional development schools. *The Elementary School Journal, 96*(1), 87–106. https://doi.org/10.1086/461816

Darling-Hammond, L., & Ducommun, C.E. (2010). *Recognizing and developing effective teaching: What policy makers should know and do* [Policy brief]. National Education Association and American Association of Colleges for Teacher Education. http://www.nea.org/assets/docs/HE/Effective_Teaching_-_Linda_Darling-Hammond.pdf

Darling-Hammond, L., Flook, L., Cook-Harvey, C., Barron, B., & Osher, D. (2019). Implications for the educational practice of the science of learning and development. *Applied Developmental Science*, 1–44. https://doi.org/10.1080/10888691.2018.1537791

Darling-Hammond, L., Hyler, M.E., & Gardner, M. (2017). *Effective teacher professional development.* Learning Policy Institute. https://learningpolicyinstitute.org/sites/default/files/product-files/Effective_Teacher_Professional_Development_REPORT.pdf

Dozier, T.K. (2007). Turning good teachers into great leaders. *Educational Leadership, 65*(1), 54–59.

Freeman, R., Miller, D., & Newcomer, L. (2015). Integration of academic and behavioral MTSS at the district level using implementation science. *Learning Disabilities: A Contemporary Journal, 13*(1), 59–72.

Guckert, M., Mastropieri, M.A., & Scruggs, T.E. (2016). Personalizing research: Special educators' awareness of evidence-based practice. *Exceptionality, 24*(2), 63–78. https://doi.org/10.1080/09362835.2014.986607

Hagaman, J.L., & Casey, K.J. (2018). Teacher attrition in special education: Perspectives from the field. *Teacher Education and Special Education, 41*(4), 277–291. https://doi.org/10.1177/0888406417725797

Holdheide, L.R., Goe, L., Croft, A., & Reschly, D.J. (2010). *Challenges in Evaluating Special Education Teachers and English Language Learner Specialists* [Research & Policy Brief]. National Comprehensive Center for Teacher Quality.

Johnson, S.M., & Donaldson, M.L. (2007). Overcoming the obstacles to leadership. *Educational Leadership, 65*(1), 8–13.

Jones, L., Stall, G., & Yarbrough, D. (2013). The importance of professional learning communities for school improvement. *Creative Education, 4*(05), 357.

Kennedy, J.F. (1963). Remarks Prepared for Delivery at the Trade Mart in Dallas, November 22, 1963. *Public Papers of the Presidents of the United States, John F. Kennedy, Containing the Public Messages, Speeches, and Statements of the President, 1963.* Retrieved from https://www.jfklibrary.org/archives/other-resources/john-f-kennedy-speeches/dallas-tx-trade-mart-undelivered-19631122

Kohm, B., & Nance, B. (2009). Creating collaborative cultures. *Educational Leadership, 67*(2), 67–72.

Langher, V., Caputo, A., & Ricci, M.E. (2017). The potential role of perceived support for reduction of special education teachers' burnout. *International Journal of Educational Psychology, 6*(2), 120–147. https://doi.org/10.17583/ijep.2017.2126

Leko, M.M., Brownell, M.T., Sindelar, P.T., & Kiely, M.T. (2015). Envisioning the future of special education personnel preparation in a standards-based era. *Exceptional Children, 82*(1), 25–43. https://doi.org/10.1177/0014402915598782

Lignugaris/Kraft, B., Sindelar, P.T., McCray, E.D., & Kimerling, J. (2014). The "wicked question" of teacher education effects and what to do about it. In P.T. Sindelar, E.D. McCray, M.T. Brownell, & B. Lignugaris/Kraft (Eds.), *Handbook of research on special education teacher preparation* (pp. 489–499). Routledge. https://doi.org/10.4324/9780203817032.ch27

Liston, D., Borko, H., & Whitcomb, J. (2008). The teacher educator's role in enhancing teacher quality. *Journal of Teacher Education, 59*(20), 111–116. https://doi.org/10.1177/0022487108315581

McLeskey, J., Barringer, M.-D., Billingsley, B., Brownell, M., Jackson, D., Kennedy, M., Lewis, T., Maheady, L., Rodriguez, J., Scheeler, M.C., Winn, J., & Ziegler, D. (2017, January). *High-leverage practices in special education.* Council for Exceptional Children & CEEDAR Center.

Minnici, A. (2014). The mind shift in teacher evaluation: Where we stand and where we need to go. *American Educator, 38*(1), 22–26.

Mulford, B. (2003). *School leaders: Changing roles and impact on teacher and school effectiveness.* Education and Training Policy Division, OECD.

Pont, B., Nusche, D., & Moorman, H. (2008). *Improving school leadership, Volume 1: Policy and practice.* OCED Publishing. https://doi.org/10.1787/9789264044715-en

Pretorius, S.G. (2012). The implications of teacher effectiveness requirements for initial teacher education reform. *Journal of Social Sciences, 34*(3), 310–317. https://doi.org/10.3844/jssp.2012.310.317

Reeves, T.D., & Lowenhaupt, R.J. (2016). Teachers as leaders: Pre-service teachers' aspirations and motivations. *Teaching and Teacher Education, 57,* 176–187. https://doi.org/10.1016/j.tate.2016.03.011

Rock, M.L., Spooner, F., Nagro, S., Vasquez, E., Dunn, C., Leko, M., Luckner, J., Bausch, M., Donehower, C., & Jones, J.L. (2016). 21st century change drivers: Considerations for constructing transformative models of special education teacher development. *Teacher Education and Special Education, 39*(2), 98–120. https://doi.org/10.1177/0888406416640634

Scheeler, M.C., Budin, S., & Markelz, A. (2016). The role of teacher preparation in promoting evidence-based practice in schools. *Learning Disabilities: A Contemporary Journal, 14*(2), 171–187.

Sharp, L.A., Simmons, M., Goode, F., & Scott, L. (2019). Enhance and extend preservice special educators' learning with curricular content knowledge. *SRATE Journal, 28*(1), 52–60.

Shepherd, K.G., Fowler, S., McCormick, J., Wilson, C.L., & Morgan, D. (2016). The search for role clarity: Challenges and implications for special education teacher preparation. *Teacher Education and Special Education, 39*(2), 83–97. https://doi.org/10.1177/0888406416637904

Shin, M., Lee, H., & McKenna, J.W. (2016). Special education and general education preservice teachers' co-teaching experiences: A comparative synthesis of qualitative research. *International Journal of Inclusive Education, 20*(1), 91–107. https://doi.org/10.1080/13603116.2015.1074732

Slanda, D. (2017). *Role ambiguity: Defining the elusive role of the special education teacher who works in inclusive settings* [Doctoral dissertation]. University of Central Florida STARS. https://stars.library.ucf.edu/etd/5563

Spillane, J.P., Diamond, J.P., Sherer, J.Z., & Coldren, A.F. (2004). Distributing leadership. In M.J. Coles & G. Southworth (Eds.), *Distributing leadership: Creating the schools of tomorrow* (pp. 37–49). Open University Press.

Teacher Leadership Exploratory Consortium. (2011). *Teacher leader model standards.* National Education Association. http://www.nea.org/assets/docs/TeacherLeaderModel Standards2011.pdf

Vittek, J.E. (2015). Promoting special educator teacher retention: A critical review of the literature. *Sage Open, 5*(2). https://doi.org/10.1177/2158244015589994

Wang, M.T., & Degol, J.L. (2016). School climate: A review of the construct, measurement, and impact on student outcomes. *Educational Psychology Review, 28*(2), 315–352. https://doi.org/10.1007/s10648-015-9319-1

Welch, J., & Welch, S. (2005). *Winning.* Harper Business.

Whitaker, M.C., & Valtierra, K.M. (2018). Enhancing preservice teachers' motivation to teach diverse learners. *Teaching and Teacher Education, 73*, 171–182. https://doi.org/10.1016/j.tate.2018.04.004

White, M.E., Makkonen, R., & Stewart, K.B. (2009). *A multistate review of professional teaching standards* (Issues & Answers, REL 2009-No. 075). U.S. Department of Education, Institute of Education Sciences, National Center for Education Evaluation and Regional Assistance, Regional Educational Laboratory West. http://ies.ed.gov/ncee/edlabs

# 2

# TEACHER LEADERSHIP

## Amanda Passmore, Cristina Salvador, and Catrina Dorsey

The school administrator at Adams Elementary is considering teachers to serve on the building's instructional leadership team for the upcoming school year.

| Administrator's Perspective | Special Educator's Perspective |
|---|---|
| I would like Ms. Kamp, the third-grade reading teacher, to join our building leadership team. She has been with the school for 3 years now and had the highest scores on the state reading test. She is also well liked by the staff and should fit well into the existing team. My hope is that she can translate the success she has had in third-grade reading to all other grades at our school. | I've been at Adams 7 years now and feel like I am constantly being overlooked for a leadership role. I know I have a lot to contribute. I have worked with the majority of teachers and in a variety of subject areas. My students have always shown strong academic growth. I could use the success I have seen in progress monitoring and differentiation to support the learning of all students at Adams in addition to those with IEPs. |

**Key Points:**

- Understand **why** the inclusion of special educators is valuable to school leadership models.
- Identify specific **skills** special educators possess that make them ideal teacher leaders for your school.

- Identify ways to **overcome** limitations that may contribute to the under-representation of special educators as leaders.
- Identify various leadership models to continue to **grow and develop** an effective inclusive school that leverages the expertise of the special educator.
- Determine ways to **utilize** special educators in leadership roles that will contribute to inclusive academic, behavioral, and collaborative practices that also support student achievement.

The role of an administrator involves a complex myriad of management duties that tend to 'snowball' in quantity, leaving administrators to rely on the reciprocal relationship of teacher leaders as a way to manage their shared vision for instruction. The concept of teacher leadership has become an integral component of education reform in recent years. The composition of school-level leadership teams is instrumental in establishing a productive climate and culture that promotes student achievement. Schools that maintain an increased capacity for teacher leadership also display substantially higher student achievement in both math and English language arts than schools with lower levels of teacher leadership (Ingersoll et al., 2018).

Beginning in the 1980s, teacher leadership was rooted in small-scale collaboration related to a specific teaching context. Today, teacher leadership has expanded to become an integral part of whole school reform due to the realization that teacher expertise is an important factor in improving educational practices that will ultimately impact student achievement. The definition of leadership has equally expanded to incorporate both formal and informal roles that can take place inside and outside the classroom. In all cases, the assumption is that teacher leadership seeks to capitalize on the individual strengths of designated teachers in order to meet the academic, behavioral, and collaborative needs of a school or district. The title of teacher leader honors both the educators' role in the classroom as well as individual levels of expertise in their capacity as a school leader. Ultimately, the term teacher leader marries the two roles teachers are simultaneously engaging in, teacher and leader.

The role of a teacher leader can work in tandem with a school or district leader whose obligations do not encompass daily responsibilities at the classroom level. Teacher leaders are able to incorporate a lens that considers the classroom-level responsibilities of a school. This lens allows a teacher leader to refine context-specific instructional and behavioral practices, while also modeling and collaborating with their peers (Curtis, 2013). This is essential in a school community where there is something uniquely impactful when a leader is also a peer with the same job obligations as a recipient of that leadership. In the context of a school, a teacher as a leader is better able to understand the nuances, setting, and needs of a classroom teacher. For this reason, a teacher leader's voice not only provides context for district and school leaders' decision-making, but also other teachers at the ground level. Teacher leaders serve as a bridge for communication between leaders and staff, who are impacted by the implementation of school-wide initiatives. In turn, veteran teachers are often tapped for the role of a teacher leader. Often the first teachers to be considered for teacher leadership roles are those in a more traditional, general education role. While these teachers should be included and are vital to school leadership, a truly successful model of teacher leadership includes teachers with varying levels of experience as a way to enhance a school or district's ability to support the needs of every student in their population.

Historically, the unique knowledge and initiative of the special educator has not been often considered in the selection of teacher leaders (Billingsley, 2007). This is due to a variety of reasons, including uncertainty of how to capitalize on their skills within a school-wide lens or a misunderstanding of their knowledge set altogether. This reality has created a lack of special education representation within the teacher leadership landscape, which has consequently impacted the promotion of an inclusive school environment. To leverage the structures of teacher leadership, district and school leaders should consider how special educators can fit into their existing leadership structures.

---

**STOP AND REFLECT**

When you think of the leadership structures or roles in your school or district:

1. How can these roles best utilize the instructional strengths and areas of expertise of special educators?
2. What new roles could be created to leverage the expertise of special educators at your school or district?

---

## The Benefits of Special Educators as Teacher Leaders

The impact of teacher leadership on student achievement is 'second only to classroom instruction' (Leithwood et al., 2004, p. 5). There is a plethora of factors related to teacher leadership that have an impact on student achievement. At the school level, the incorporation of teacher leadership can increase staff morale, contributing to positive classroom interactions that encourage risk taking and innovation. Teacher leadership has been shown to impact teacher retention, job satisfaction, and the development of one's own professional identity. This can be particularly important for special educators who experience high levels of teacher turnover resulting in increased recruitment needs by schools and districts.

The recent paradigm shift toward creating school environments that foster inclusion has created an even greater need for the representation of special educators in leadership teams that determine school-wide instructional decisions. School-wide inclusive practices have been a relatively quick shift in mindset for many schools. In fact, it was not until the United States passage of Public Law 94-142 in 1975 that students with significant disabilities were required to receive any sort of public education at all. To address the shift toward inclusion, special educators have typically been delegated to oversee legal or compliance-related tasks in lieu of instructional leadership roles. However, these types of roles do not contribute to the distribution of instructional, behavioral, and collaborative expertise needed to promote an inclusive school culture. When special educators are segregated and devalued within a school culture in terms of teacher leadership, their students are likely to be as well (Billingsley, 2007). Teachers and staff notice when special educators are not represented at the leadership level of a school. This inadvertently creates the assumption that a school's instructional focus is not inclusive of students with Individual Education Plans (IEPs) and the education of students receiving those services are not a priority either. This reality has major implications in creating a truly inclusive school environment. The active involvement of special educators in school systems is the only way for inclusive practices to take root and communicate that the education of all students is of utmost priority. Ultimately, the involvement and dedication of individuals at *all* levels and within *all* contexts of the school system are needed for a change to take hold.

Inclusive academic, behavioral, and collaborative practices do not exclusively benefit students with disabilities. General educators have historically not been adequately prepared for the increased diversity of needs seen in schools today. In recent years, researchers and practitioners have promoted differentiated instruction to account for individual learning styles and the diversity seen in today's classrooms. However, while teachers acknowledge the need for differentiated instruction, many admit that they rarely have the time or knowledge to apply differentiation effectively within their instructional practice (Valiandes & Neophytou, 2018). This may be a result of general educators' tendency to focus on the instructional practices that target the whole group. Consequently, many general education teachers rely on special educators as informal leaders when it comes to the ideas of individual student-focused instruction. The unique skills special educators' have related to differentiation, progress monitoring, behavioral supports, and problem solving associated with individual student needs have the potential to benefit *all* students. This includes those students in general education settings where teachers may have fewer strategies and experiences that promote individualized planning (Zigmond & Kloo, 2017). The incorporation of special educators as teacher leaders has the potential to have a significant impact on an entire school's inclusive culture and climate in a fundamental way.

---

**STOP AND REFLECT**

Important questions to consider when evaluating the use of your school's inclusive practices:

1. What are areas of growth and/or priorities for your school in terms of inclusive practices?
2. What shifts and supports are necessary to achieve these goals? Consider both educators' skills and beliefs around inclusive practices.

---

## How the Skills of a Special Educator Translate to Proficient Leadership

It may be assumed that the skills of a strong practitioner naturally translate to the responsibilities and skills required to be an influential teacher leader. This is rarely the case, as many educators require development in skills associated with school-wide leadership (York-Barr & Duke, 2004). These skills include group management, collaboration, communication, strategic planning, and big picture thinking. Many newly appointed teacher leaders quickly realize leading adults requires a significantly different skill set than the one used with students. This may lower their potential for influence when it comes to school outcomes enhanced through teacher leadership.

Special educators, on the other hand, are uniquely positioned to acquire skills related to school-wide leadership. This is because leadership skills directly align to many of the roles they currently take on as special educators. Special educators collaborate, communicate, and rely on conflict negotiation skills daily when working with parents, co-teachers, paraprofessionals, and various other educational partners. These types of adult partnerships and responsibilities in leadership are a natural part of special educator's instructional responsibilities. Few teachers assume a supervisory role, but special educators shoulder this responsibility when it comes to managing special education support staff members. This relationship involves a level of mentorship, organizational management, and relationship building to promote mutual trust and respect. Special educators also have experience envisioning a big picture when planning and managing its implementation through organizational analysis. When writing an IEP a special educator must use data to create an end-of-year goal using the SMART criteria (specific, measurable, attainable, results oriented, and timely) in addition to periodic benchmarks throughout the year to achieve and monitor the progress of that goal. Breaking down a big goal into achievable steps and using data to evaluate progress along the way is a natural way of thinking for a special educator. These experiences in systematic planning can directly contribute to the thinking needed in the creation and implementation of a school-wide initiative or priority.

Overall, many skills that need to be cultivated in teacher leaders are inherent in work that special educators engage in. These are skills a special educator has learned through their teacher preparation programs and further homed in their practices at the school level (see Table 2.1). As the role of administrators becomes more complex, having teacher leaders that already

**Table 2.1** Teacher Leadership Skills: Connection of Special Educators' Skills and Experiences

| Needs of a teacher leader | Connection to special education teacher skills and experiences |
| --- | --- |
| Work collaboratively and build trust with colleagues | • Experience co-teaching and planning with general education providers<br>• Management and organization of special education support staff<br>• Collaboration with IEP team and service providers<br>• Collaboration with parents/guardians of students with IEPs |
| Support and promote growth among colleagues | • Unofficial leaders in the area of differentiation<br>• School resource for specialized learning supports<br>• School models for behavior supports and interventions<br>• Resource for problem solving and adapting curriculum |
| Communicate effectively and listen to others | • Frequent communication with service providers and paraprofessionals<br>• Ongoing communication with families and caregivers<br>• Collaborative communication with general education providers<br>• Listening to input of IEP team and families when educating students |
| Handle and mediate conflict | • Experience with negotiating and mediating during IEP meeting<br>• Skills in advocacy related to the needs of students and their families<br>• Experience navigating conflict with coteachers or paraprofessionals<br>• Resolving issues related to service delivery of students with IEPs |

(*Continued*)

**Table 2.1**  Teacher Leadership Skills: Connection of Special Educators' Skills and Experiences (*Continued*)

| Needs of a teacher leader | Connection to special education teacher skills and experiences |
|---|---|
| Effective in group processing skills | • Experience planning for a variety of grade levels and abilities<br>• Experience differentiation through planning for various learning styles<br>• Experience in group problem solving as IEP team member<br>• Advocating, when needed, for students with special needs |
| Assess, interpret, and prioritize needs and concerns | • Implements federal requirements related to IEP within various settings<br>• Prioritizes learning goals for students with disabilities<br>• Utilizes expertise to provide accessible instruction<br>• Mediates teacher concerns for placement and supports |
| Solid understanding of organizational 'big picture' | • Daily data collection and analysis to aid in responsive instruction<br>• Utilization of data to develop and implement long-term IEP goals<br>• Utilization of data for development and implementation of IEP goals<br>• Experienced alignment and creation of benchmarks for annual goals<br>• Ensuring access to grade-level content for students with IEPs |

Adapted from York-Barr and Duke (2004).

demonstrate the skills necessary to contribute to a school-wide leadership role would be a welcomed addition.

---

**STOP AND REFLECT**

Review Table 2.1 outlining the skills needed when assuming the role of a teacher leader (York-Barr & Duke, 2004).

Ask yourself:

1. What are some of the skills listed that resonate with the special education teachers you have in your building or district?
2. What challenges are you anticipating when utilizing special education teachers as leaders?

## Distributing Leadership to Allow for Inclusion of Special Educator and Their Strengths

No successful school can be led solely by an individual. The concept and benefits associated with teacher leadership align to models of distributed leadership (Harris, 2005; Muijs & Harris, 2003). Successful schools ensure that leadership is distributed across individuals and the most successful schools seek equal representation and perspectives from all teachers and stakeholders. Distributing leadership leverages the expertise of various individuals and ensures the effective dissemination of important initiatives at the center of school improvement. Distributed leadership is not the handing off of unwanted task or initiatives. When this is the case, educators in a leadership community find themselves unmotivated and uninspired. Often times this is seen as special educators being tasked with legal compliancy or general educators taking on micromanaging of their peers. A successful distribution of leadership allows teacher leaders the opportunity to invest in areas of personal importance while also ensuring the success of all students. Distributed leadership is not about increasing the number of leaders in a school; instead, it focuses on increasing the leadership qualities and capabilities of individuals in a school or district (Harris, 2013). Nowhere is distributed leadership more important than in the initiatives associated with inclusive school practices.

Researchers have identified three types of distribution of leadership (Spillane et al., 2004): Collaborated, collective, and coordinated distribution. All three of these models support district and school structure. In various types of work, a particular model may be better suited for an individual district, school, leader, or teacher leader. Additionally, various initiatives may lend themselves to a specific structure; therefore, leaders should consider their own style and school when selecting a model of distributed leadership (see Table 2.2).

### *Collaborated Distribution*

In this model, work on the same goal, project, or routine is stretched over two or more individuals who operate together. Collaborated distribution requires leaders come together in the same place and time to work collectively on a given goal in a way that allows leaders to be interdependent as they coperform a leadership role. Collaborated distribution is often seen in schools when teachers work on committees, curriculum, or teacher development. In all these activities, the special educator's point of view in conjunction with the traditional teacher's would be beneficial to ensure all students have access to all services and initiatives. If a new curriculum is being developed, the special educator can provide context for differentiation that

**Table 2.2** Distribution of Leadership Models

| Distributed leadership model | Definition | Considerations |
|---|---|---|
| Collaborated distribution | Work is stretched over two or more individuals who work together to execute the same goal, project, task, or routine while working interdependent of one another | • Do time allocations allow for team collaboration?<br>• What are expectations for communication?<br>• What specific team norms have been established?<br>• Does the team have representation from all stakeholders?<br>• Will the administrator be an active member or supervisor? |
| Collective distribution | Work is stretched over two or more leaders who work separately yet interdependently on the same goal, project, task, or routine | • What are expectations for communication?<br>• How will the team come together to calibrate?<br>• How will roles be established?<br>• How will the individual pieces align to the big picture goal?<br>• Does the team have representation from all stakeholders?<br>• What is the role of each stakeholder?<br>• Do all members have the same or different roles?<br>• Will the administrator be an active member or supervisor? |
| Coordinated distribution | Work and activities are performed in a particular sequence where individuals work either separately or together on the same goal, project, task, or routine | • Will the team work collaboratively or collectively?<br>• What deadlines will be established?<br>• What are expectations for communication?<br>• Does the team have representation from all stakeholders?<br>• Do all members have the same or different roles or tasks?<br>• How will the individual pieces align to the end goal? |

Adapted from Spillane et al., 2004.

will support not only their students, but also other struggling students. An administrator would be hard pressed to find a school-wide goal where the unique perspective of the special educator would not lend itself to the benefit of all students, teachers, or staff. When developing a collaborated distribution team, a leader should always ensure a representative from the general and special education populations of their school or district.

## Collective Distribution

When work is stretched over two or more leaders who are working separately yet interdependently on the same goal, task, or initiative they are engaging in a collective distribution model. Tasks involved in collective distribution allow for evaluation of instructional implementation or coaching. This is because roles such as coaching or mentoring are done in pairs across various leaders who are working toward the same overarching initiative. Another example may be seen in a group of leaders evaluating the implementation of universal Positive Behavior Interventions and Supports (PBIS) through conducting walk-throughs as individuals then contributing to a shared database utilizing a common observation protocol. In this model, there may be times when individual leaders come together to calibrate and discuss trends of their own individual work. The benefit of this model is the option for leaders to work within their own availability, in specific context, or areas of interest. Often in these scenarios of distributed leadership special educators are evaluated or supported by individuals lacking a full understanding of the needs of their student population and/ or the legal requirements related to their position. Additionally, a general education teacher may need the lens of special educator to support in these same areas as they work to provide an inclusive environment that educates students with disabilities. In this sense, collective distribution can support one-to-one pairings based on teacher roles, but it can also lend itself to various combinations of roles to broaden the perspectives of both teachers and leaders.

## Coordinated Distribution

The model of coordinated distribution lends itself to leadership routines that require activities be performed in a particular sequence. At the school level, this may look like the implementation of a data analysis protocol, coordination of school-wide assessments, implementation of Multi-Tiered Systems of Supports (MTSS), or PBIS. For more information on MTSS or PBIS see chapter resources in Appendix B. In addition to the reiteration of knowledge special educators and traditional teacher leaders can naturally bring to these types of teams, the special educators' big picture thinking and ability to break outcomes into manageable tasks are ideal for this leadership model. Having the special educator involved in these leadership outcomes allows schools to incorporate their strengths toward the benefit of a school or district to ensure that large-scale projects, goals, or task are realized. For this type of model, the logistics encompassed in the sequence of activities are essential. To ensure that all details are accounted for a well-rounded team of leaders needs to be considered.

Ultimately, the models of leadership distribution need not operate in silos. Depending on the task a team may rely on a combination of these models. More importantly when considering these types of leadership structures, school leaders ensure that a voice from both special and general education is present and that all relevant stakeholders are given a seat at the table. Without these considerations, schools risk not only isolating their special education population, but denying access of special supports that would impact the progress of all students and teachers. In addition, not all teacher leaders may be well suited for the outcomes associated with a given model or task. For this reason, a successful school leader considers both the needs of the task and the model to ensure a positive outcome. These considerations will fundamentally support *all* students impacted by these initiatives, goals, and tasks.

---

**STOP AND REFLECT**

After reviewing the types of distributed leadership models (Table 2.2). Consider the following questions as they relate to your own school or district's models of leadership:

1. What is a current task or future initiative related to your school or district?
2. What distributed leadership model would best support that intended outcome? Consider the specific strengths of your district, school, and leadership.
3. What unique points of view would benefit that model and outcome? Think of both your general education teachers and special educators.

---

## Reducing Limitations to Create Opportunities for Leadership Among Special Educators

Superficial obstacles have often contributed to the underrepresentation of special educators in school-wide leadership roles. These obstacles have been perpetuated by assumptions and a lack of strategies to overcome them. Both administrators and special educators have been hindered by perceived obstacles to teacher leadership; thus, shifts in mindset and potential strategies can help navigate a means to overcome them. In thinking about leadership, there are four areas that typically need to be addressed.

## Student Demographics

It is often assumed that the students that make up the demographics of a special education teachers' caseload do not translate to the general education population at the school level. This is an outdated misconception. As previously stated, special educators are expert practitioners in the areas of differentiation, adaptation, data collection, behavior supports, progress monitoring, and problem solving. Not only are these skills beneficial to *all* teachers and students, but they are also central to education reform and inclusive practices.

Special educators are highly skilled in individualized student supports in both academics and behavior. Individualization is something that all students need to be successful. It goes without saying, a student does not need to have an IEP to benefit from evidence-based practices and individualized supports. The push for inclusion is not limited to placement. It is about allocating resources to meet the needs of students through the incorporation of inclusive practices at every level of a school's vision. In this sense, limiting a special educators' impact to solely the students with IEPs does not capitalize on the skills special educators have that could impact all students in a school's population of diverse learners. Every student is first and foremost a general education student. Having an IEP does not mean a student needs something entirely different than their grade-level peers. A disability status is not about placement, it is about a continuum at all levels of services provided at the school level. When schools view the education of special education students as a responsibility belonging to *all* teachers, they can begin to capitalize on the resources and expertise of special educators.

## Lack of Content Expertise

There is a tendency for schools to group teachers by content and/or grade level. Adherence to this structure is an outdated practice that compromises the principles of inclusion and denies general educators access to interdisciplinary collaboration on a regular basis. It leaves special educators as outliers to the traditional structures of collaboration. Many special educators can relate to being excluded from content team meetings or school-wide professional development under the premise that 'it did not apply to them.' This is not only denying students with IEPs access to grade-level instructional practices, but it is also diminishing special educators' collaborative role in the development of content that may support students in mainstream classrooms. For example, many of the strategies special educators utilize when working with nonverbal disability populations can also support students who are English learners. By assuming special educators lack content expertise, schools are actually denying all teachers access to interdisciplinary collaborative relationships that could actually enhance content.

Special educators are also versed in various grade levels and content areas. Teaching assignments based on the needs and makeup of students receiving specialized services often requires special educators to loop grade levels on a yearly basis. The benefit in this is the special educator's ability to see both vertical and horizontal alignment within curricula. Engagement in multiple content areas allows special educators to create more authentic learning opportunities across content areas. Skills being taught in science can be reinforced in literacy and math as a result of these cross-content collaborations happening on a daily basis. Very few teachers have the opportunity to develop such a vast understanding of learning trajectories, but it is something that special educators embrace daily. Thus, a special educator's ability to view potential initiatives critically through multiple lenses can have positive implications for school-wide instructional planning.

Aside from content, special educators are experts in the area of behavioral practices. Their preservice preparation allocates time for courses rich in evidence-based behavioral analyses and supports as compared to teachers in other content areas. Therefore, special educators are qualified to lead and support best practices when it comes to behavior management, incentives, and function-based interventions. These are skills that all teachers require considering a quarter of teachers cite student discipline issues as their greatest contributor to stress and increased inclination to leave the profession altogether (Ingersoll, 2007). Special educators' knowledge in individualized behavior practices and multitier supports could help address the behavior management challenges that many teachers face daily. The assumption that special educators are void of 'content' expertise rejects the breadth of their unique skill set related to both behavioral and instructional experiences.

## Time Constraints

Time is a barrier that all teacher leaders face. However, this assumption is often compounded for the special educator who is seen to have additional responsibilities aside from a teacher leader in a more traditional role. The job of a special educator involves roles and responsibilities that extend outside classroom planning and instruction. These tasks include collaboration with teachers, service providers, and parents as well as the development of IEPs, daily progress monitoring, and fostering the development of transitional skills among other things. The good news is that the strategies special educators have developed to manage the dynamic undertakings of their instructional role also translate to the workings of a school-wide teacher leader.

Oftentimes, due to the multiple roles that special educators are already responsible for, concerns about time constraints may lead to their hesitancy to take on the role of teacher leader. The assumption is that undertaking a leadership role will undermine their ability to successfully manage their job as special educators.

To overcome this, administrators must show sensitivity by ensuring support in managing these dual roles as a teacher and teacher leader. This assurance could take the form of a confidant who can also relate to the stresses of having a multifaceted job or involve more concrete supports to aid a special educator in time management. These types of supports could be an additional preparation period, reduction in caseload, or a stipend for time spent outside their classroom duties. An administrator may find that a special educator has the ability to open-up creative pathways to support time management across the school organization that could aid in collaboration, communication, and inclusive planning practices. Special education leadership representation in a school can enhance the school-wide inclusive practices, allowing others in the school community to shoulder the weight and responsibility often thrust upon the special educator. These solutions may reduce initially perceived limitations related to time and make the special educator feel more comfortable assuming a leadership role. In the end, it all starts with an administrator acknowledging the feelings a special educator may have when being asked to take on a leadership role. By further communicating confidence in their expertise, administrators can begin to overcome this potential roadblock and work toward enhancing the climate and culture of the school around inclusive practices.

## Lack of Understanding of Special Education

Administrators tend to know and interact more with the legal aspects of special education, whereas special educators understand more regarding implementation at an academic and behavioral level. Having these distinct points of view can often limit an administrator's potential to see special education concepts as related to school-wide initiatives. Collaboration with a special education teacher leader can increase the content gaps many administrators may or may not know they have around special education instructional practices. These gaps in understanding can often lead to misconceptions in the roll out of special education initiatives, undermining the initial intent of an initiative such as improving inclusive practices (Crockett, 2002). An unperceived gap in instructional knowledge on the part of school administration has often led to leadership focused on compliance tasks and less on promoting effective partnerships that support inclusive student learning. There is a misconception that inclusion is the practice of moving students with IEPs from one setting to another when in fact it concerns a shift in school-wide systems at the instructional and intervention levels.

Additionally, there is a need for new special educators to be supported instructionally by a fellow special educator. Special educators new to the profession identified fellow special educators as their greatest resource to improved instruction, however many of these new teachers were not provided a mentor with this context-related experience (Billingsley et al., 2004). Additionally, many special educators do not feel included in school-wide professional learning or feel that it lacks opportunities to promote their growth as special educators. Having the voice of a special educator as a leadership partner can help address the needs of special educators in terms of instructional coaching, mentorship, and professional learning. Leadership actions that capitalize on the knowledge of special educators and push teachers to continue to grow their practice will promote the job satisfaction of fellow special educators while simultaneously contributing value to the learning of all teachers.

Other administrators or district leaders may feel overwhelmed by the vast legal and clinical jargon associated with special education. Leading many to feel inadequately prepared to address behavioral or academic needs of students with special needs due to gaps in their own principal preparation programs. For these reasons, leaders may inadvertently shy away from interactions with special educators at a leadership level. This would be a mistake. In reality, it is impossible for a school or district leader to know everything needed for superior instruction. An effective leader relies on the expertise of others and the same should be done for special education. Distributed leadership is a perfect place to start this process since it allows teacher leaders to share their expertise with the school and leadership community.

---

### STOP AND REFLECT

As you begin to think about special education within your school or district's teacher leadership structures consider the following:

1. What is an area of need in your own leadership that you believe the perspective of a special educator could help address?
2. What obstacles do you anticipate in implementing a leadership model that is inclusive of special educators? Do you have an initial idea of how to address these obstacles?
3. Who is a key special education stakeholder(s) you could look to for input in implementing inclusive practices and enhancing your school or district's initiatives?

## Implementing Special Education Leadership at the School and District Level

Ultimately, when an administrator sees value in the knowledge and expertise a special educator can contribute to their school, they will find ways to remove barriers and promote these teachers' leadership capacities. When determining a path for special education leadership, an administrator should consider two things:

1. What are the needs of my school community in terms of academics, behavior, and interdisciplinary collaboration?
2. What strengths do I see in my special education staff and how can I promote their strengths through teacher leadership in one or more of these areas?

To begin to think about these pathway questions is first important to think about the needs of your school or district using the provided **Systematic Inclusive Practices Planning and Implementation Matrix** (Table 2.3).

---

### STOP AND REFLECT

**Step 1** Think about the needs of your school community. Complete the following matrix in Table 2.3 to identify needs related to academics, behavior, and interdisciplinary collaboration at the schoolwide, instructional, and intervention levels, keeping in mind inclusive practices.

See a sample completed matrix in the implementation resources within Appendix B.

---

The subsequent chapters of the book will outline key traits of special educators that lend themselves to inclusive school-wide instructional and intervention practices. These roles, whether formal or informal in nature, can capitalize on the individual strengths of every special educator in a building. This incorporation will contribute to the creation and sustainability of an inclusive school culture.

Table 2.3 Systematic Inclusive Practices Planning and Implementation Matrix

|  | Academics | Behavior | Interdisciplinary collaboration |
|---|---|---|---|
| School-wide systems |  |  |  |
| Instruction |  |  |  |
| Intervention |  |  |  |

Adapted from OSEP presentation (as cited in Quirk, 2018).

## STOP AND REFLECT

**Step 2** Consider the following list of upcoming topics in subsequent chapters and determine which may correspond to some of the needs you identified for your school community.

| Chapter | Topic | Description and characteristics |
|---------|-------|-------------------------------|
| 3 | Data Expertise | Expertise in collecting and analyzing data to inform schoolwide, grade-level, classroom, and student-level needs along with potential solutions |
| 4 | Expertise in Data-Based Individualization | Experience in a method of ensuring that students displaying challenging behavior and learning needs make progress through the utilization of evidence-based interventions and supports |
| 5 | Adaptive Expertise | Expertise in a problem-solving process emphasizing the creation of new knowledge and procedures to effectively combat problems and novel situations |
| 6 | Instructional Expertise | Expertise in characteristics that ensure educators are able to promote learning and engagement among a variety of students in multiple domains related to student outcomes |
| 7 | Expertise in Collaboration | Experience related to fostering positive interactions within a group or among a variety of individuals, to accomplish a shared goal related to various activities and task |
| 8 | Expertise in Advocacy | Internalization of the disposition, skills, and knowledge necessary to bring about change on behalf of oneself or others |

Additionally, it is recommended that a designated school-wide leadership team have at least one special educator represented in its members since creating an inclusive school starts with special education representation within those leadership structures (see Table 2.4). The voice and reciprocal relationship of a special educator representative is essential for a school to take on inclusive school practices.

---

**STOP AND REFLECT**

**Step 3** Review the following potential special education teacher leadership roles in Table 2.4. Based on the needs identified in your matrix from **Step 1** and the strengths/expertise of your current special educators, what roles best suit the current needs of your school?

---

Table 2.4 Potential Areas and Roles in Teacher Leadership for Special Educators

| Potential leadership roles | Skills required and potential areas of influence |
|---|---|
| **Formal appointed leadership positions** | |
| Building leadership/ Administrative team member | • Provide special education lens to building initiatives and contribute to 'big picture' thinking<br>• Provide insight related to data, behavior, instruction, etc. to support *all* students<br>• Identify and support program needs for professional development that is inclusive of all students<br>• Establish norms around issues related to diverse learners (e.g., coteaching and collaboration)<br>• Support development and dispersion of resources to support initiative in inclusive practices |
| School-wide special education coordinator | • Advocate for students with disabilities and their families within the school community<br>• Serve as a representative for special education teachers, support staff, and paraprofessionals<br>• Provide insight and support toward schoolwide scheduling in regard to students with IEPs<br>• Assist in developing and implementing a schoolwide vision of inclusive practices |
| Department chair | • Utilize teacher-specific strengths to build capacity of special education department<br>• Lead special education teacher teams and mentor novice teachers on the team<br>• Facilitate the development and progress of special-education-specific initiatives<br>• Chair or cochair a grade-level/content team to provide insight related to supporting *all* students |

*(Continued)*

**Table 2.4** Potential Areas and Roles in Teacher Leadership for Special Educators (*Continued*)

| Potential leadership roles | Skills required and potential areas of influence |
|---|---|
| Instructional coach | • Utilize expertise in instruction and differentiation to support teachers and student achievement<br>• Serve as an expert problem solver around specific areas of need identified by teachers and staff<br>• Provide insight and resources related to MTSS Tier I and Tier II supports<br>• Utilize expertise in behavior management and interventions to support teacher learning<br>• Support teachers in progress monitoring both academic and behavioral initiatives |
| **Coordinator teacher leadership positions** | |
| MTSS/RTI/DBI coordinator | • Provide insight and resources related to academic and behavioral intervention<br>• Support in organizing and progress monitoring schoolwide and individual student data<br>• Support in writing both long- and short-term goals for students receiving MTSS Tier II supports<br>• Problem solve and utilize adaptive expertise in implementing MTSS |
| Positive behavior intervention and supports coordinator | • Support in developing schoolwide positive behavior interventions and supports (PBIS)<br>• Provide professional learning on evidence-based research related to behavioral practices<br>• Evaluate and improve on schoolwide programs in creating a positive learning environment<br>• Collect, review, and respond to schoolwide data related to behavior (e.g., discipline referrals) |
| **Specialist teacher leadership positions** | |
| Adaptation specialist | • Model lessons and lesson planning process utilizing adaptation and differentiation<br>• Provide insight on how to differentiate curricular materials, engagement, and assessment<br>• Facilitate learning around Universal Design for Learning (UDL) in all classrooms<br>• Provide supports around vertical alignment for effective scaffolding |

(*Continued*)

**Table 2.4** Potential Areas and Roles in Teacher Leadership for Special Educators (*Continued*)

| Potential leadership roles | Skills required and potential areas of influence |
|---|---|
| Behavior specialist | • Support in establishing positive learning environments that utilize positive reinforcement<br>• Provide insight on interventions for students with behavior needs<br>• Provide support in gathering data and analyses of trends to determine function of behavior<br>• Provide support and learning around the implementation of behavior plans |
| Inclusive supports specialist | • Help mentor and support coteaching teams to collaborate, plan, and deliver instruction<br>• Share resources and insights related to including students with IEP in a variety of school settings<br>• Develop teachers and staff in practices and beliefs associated with effective inclusive systems<br>• Provide insight for collaborative partnerships between teachers, paraprofessionals, and families |
| Transition specialist | • Support the embedding of transitional skills within the curriculum<br>• Improve postsecondary outcomes through strategic and targeted support<br>• Facilitate connections for students to resources within community organizations and agencies<br>• Facilitate the transition of students with IEPs between school campuses and grade levels |
| Data specialist/Data coach | • Guide the implementation of data-based individualization, data collection, and evaluation<br>• Support teachers with progress monitoring in individual or classwide areas<br>• Build teachers' capacity to be responsive to data in their day-to-day instruction<br>• Lead schoolwide data meetings and build schoolwide culture that values data in instruction |
| **Additional opportunities for leadership** | |
| Community engagement leader | • Provide insight related to creating authentic home-to-school connections<br>• Connect teachers and families with educational resources and supports in the community<br>• Assist in creating a dialogue between families, community leaders, and the school<br>• Solicit feedback from families in the community and use data to inform school practices |

(*Continued*)

**Table 2.4** Potential Areas and Roles in Teacher Leadership for Special Educators (*Continued*)

| Potential leadership roles | Skills required and potential areas of influence |
|---|---|
| Mentor teacher | • Mentor new special education teachers, paraprofessionals, coteaching pair, and/or support staff<br>• Mentor teachers on how to accommodate and support students with special education needs<br>• Provide support for IEP writing and the implementation of IEPs |
| Attend or present at state or local conference | • Gather resources on new evidence-based practices to be implemented among teachers and staff<br>• Utilize new learning and eventually seek to share this learning with the school community<br>• Gain insight into relevant special education research and initiatives to share with others |
| Presentation of professional learning | • Develop and lead sessions on areas of expertise for special educators<br>• Provide special education voice and lens in the development of schoolwide professional learning<br>• Lead a professional learning community or book around a topic of interest<br>• Plan and implement an action research project that can be shared to promote student learning |

## Summary

The successful implementation of inclusive school practices begins with embedding special educators in the structure of teacher leadership at the school level. For inclusive systems in academics, behavior, and collaboration to take root and contribute to the success of all students, school leaders need to utilize the skills and expertise of their special education teachers. Skills in adaptive expertise, instructional expertise, data, and collaboration are inherently unique to special educators due to their preservice training and field-based experiences. These skills can ultimately be leveraged through various models of distributed leadership. The obstacles that have traditionally prevented the representation of special educators at the leadership level are both superficial and easily circumvented through communication and collaboration with special education stakeholders. By first considering the needs of their school and then looking to special educators as experts in these areas, administrators can successfully create a truly inclusive climate and culture that positively impacts the academic and behavioral success of *all* students.

## Next Steps

| | |
|---|---|
| **Assess Needs** | • Reflect on your school or district's current vision or develop a vision for inclusive practices using the **Systematic Inclusive Practices Planning and Implementation Matrix** (Table 2.3).<br>• Identify this vision or initiative impacts students with disabilities. This may be done through the observation of practices and/or meeting with special education representatives. |
| **Develop a Plan** | • Utilize subsequent chapters to inform ways to leverage special educators as teacher leaders in areas that will directly support your school's needs.<br>• Discuss the potential implications of a given goal or initiative on students with disabilities with a special education representative(s) to gain their input towards a plan. |
| **Take Action** | • Incorporate special education teacher leader's areas of strength, expertise, and experiences into the plan to ensure your school or district's vision or goal is met sufficiently.<br>• Determine a leadership distribution model can be utilized with your plan to better accomplish established goals and task (Table 2.2). |
| **Monitor Progress** | • Evaluate the progress towards your school or district's vision for inclusive practice (e.g. formal assessments, observations, teacher, student, and parent feedback).<br>• Meet with a special education representative(s) to make considerations for future school leadership structures and initiatives. |

## References

Billingsley, B. S. (2007). Recognizing and supporting the critical roles of teachers in special education leadership. *Exceptionality, 15*(3), 163–176. https://doi.org/10.1080/09362830701503503

Billingsley, B., Carlson, E., & Klein, S. (2004). The working conditions and induction support of early career special educators. *Exceptional Children, 70*(3), 333–347. https://doi.org/10.1177/001440290407000305

Crockett, J. B. (2002). Special education's role in preparing responsive leaders for inclusive schools. *Remedial and Special Education, 23*(3), 157–168. https://doi.org/10.1177/07419325020230030401

Curtis, R. (2013). *Findings a new way: Leveraging teacher leadership to meet unprecedented demands.* Aspen Institute. http://www.aspendrl.org/portal/browse/DocumentDetail?documentId=1574&download

Harris, A. (2005). Teacher leadership: More than just a feel-good factor? *Leadership and policy in schools, 4*(3), 201–219. https://doi.org/10.1080/15700760500244777

Harris, A. (2013). Distributed leadership: Friend or foe? *Educational Management Administration & Leadership, 41*(5), 545–554. https://doi.org/10.1177/1741143213497635

Ingersoll, R. (2007). High turnover plagues schools. *University of Pennsylvania Scholarly Commons: GSE Publications*. Retrieved from https://repository.upenn.edu/gse_pubs/130 (Reprinted from "High turnover plagues schools," 2002, USA Today, 13A.)

Ingersoll, R. M., Sirinides, P., & Dougherty, P. (2018). Leadership matters: Teachers' roles in school decision making and school performance. *American Educator, 42*(1), 13–17.

Lambert, L. (2003). Leadership redefined: An evocative context for teacher leadership. *School Leadership and Management, 23*(4), 421–430. https://doi.org/10.1080/1363243032000150953

Leithwood, K., Louis, K. S., Anderson, S., & Wahlstrom, K. (2004). *Review of research: How leadership influences student learning*. The Wallace Foundation. https://www.wallacefoundation.org/knowledge-center/Documents/How-Leadership-Influences-Student-Learning.pdf

Muijs, D., & Harris, A. (2003). Teacher leadership – Improvement through empowerment? An overview of the literature. *Educational Management & Administration, 31*(4), 437–448. https://doi.org/10.1177/0263211x030314007

Quirk, C. (2018, July). Maryland Coalition for Inclusive Education (MCIE): Designing effective school-wide inclusive services. In S. Weigert (Moderator), *Designing effective school-wide and early childhood inclusive programs* [Symposium]. OSEP Project Directors Conference, Arlington, VA, United States.

Spillane, J., Diamond, J., Sherer, J., & Coldren, A. (2004). Distributing leadership. In M. Coles & G. Southworth (Eds.), *Distributing leadership: Creating the schools of tomorrow* (pp. 37–49). Open University Press.

Valiandes, S., & Neophytou, L. (2018). Teachers' professional development for differentiated instruction in mixed-ability classrooms: Investigating the impact of a development program on teachers' professional learning and on students' achievement. *Teacher Development, 22*(1), 123–138. https://doi.org/10.1080/13664530.2017.1338196

York-Barr, J., & Duke, K. (2004). What do we know about teacher leadership? Findings from two decades of scholarship. *Review of Educational Research, 74*(3), 255–316. https://doi.org/10.3102/00346543074003255

Zigmond, N., & Kloo, A. (2017). General and special education are (and should be) different. In J. M. Kauffman, D. P. Hallahan, & P. C. Pullen (Eds.), *Handbook of special education* (2nd ed., pp. 249–261). Routledge. https://doi.org/10.4324/9781315517698-21

# 3

# USING DATA

## Kary Zarate, Laura Kiel, and Amanda Passmore

The annual report detailing your school's yearly progress has just been released. Your school did not reach its target for expected growth, and further analysis reveals several subgroups are underachieving. You call a staff meeting to review the results and discuss next steps.

| General education teacher's perspective | Special educator's perspective |
|---|---|
| When we get results like this it always feels like teachers are to blame. Now, a new initiative will be rolled out and I will be expected to change my practice. I understand that data is important, but I do not feel confident that I am collecting it correctly. I try to bring my lower achieving students up, but do not know how much more I can do. | This data shows that there is room for growth in our instructional practices. I am wondering how students with disabilities impacted our overall school growth? It appears that both, students with and without disabilities were challenged in similar ways. I know data isn't everything, but this provides a platform for schoolwide change. |

Key Points:

- Gain a deeper **understanding of the concept of a data expert** and the skills associated with this role.

- Identify ways to **maximize the potential** of a special educator as a data expert.
- Reflect on current schoolwide data practices in order to incorporate current special educators to **foster schoolwide improvement.**
- Encourage the use of the Data Improvement Matrix **to increase family and community involvement.**

As a school administrator, academic achievement and student growth is of the highest priority. School systems across the globe use different practices to gather data on student progress. Furthermore, schools utilize student attendance, discipline referrals, medical history, grades, demographic information, and other informal sources of information as data to gauge how their current school or district is functioning. However, 'schools are largely failing to use data to transform and improve education, even though better use of data has the potential to significantly improve how educators teach children and how administrators manage schools' (New, 2016, p. 1). Data is everywhere and administrators, teachers, and families alike must be knowledgeable and comfortable using data to inform practices. As assessment has become a cornerstone of the education system, school leaders must be well versed in the capacity and capability of the correct use of schoolwide data to transform their school. Choosing appropriate forms of data to administer and collect, accurately interpreting those sources of data, and the skilled dissemination of the findings from the data to stakeholders is quite the feat. These processes are complex and administrators cannot be expected to handle all these duties on their own. Instead, administrators and school leaders can leverage the strengths of their staff to enhance the use of data within their school. In this chapter, we propose the use of a data expert, a special educator who possesses this skillset and has the temperament to instill confidence in others to use data to inform practice. Moreover, we discuss the skills required of a data expert and the ways in which the preparation of special educators match this role.

Data experts are special educators that are capable of using data to identify challenges at the school, classroom, and student level and use the data to inform solutions. Special educators by way of their teacher preparation programs, have expertise in analyzing, collecting, and disseminating data. Teachers of students with disabilities consistently use data to measure student progress as part of instructional practice in accordance with the United States federal law of Individuals with Disabilities Education Act (IDEA). IDEA describes the process and requirements for all states to create meaningful plans for students identified with disabilities called an Individualized Education Program (IEP).

**STOP AND REFLECT**

1. Which of your teachers would you consider a data expert?
2. What are the actions and qualities that make them a data expert?

Additionally, service providers like special educators are required to monitor goals and objectives in a child's IEP to determine their progress toward their yearly goals. Data on these goals is used by special educators to identify interventions or create plans for student success. These educators are comfortable with multiple sources of data collection for academic, social, and emotional skills. Special educators offer a unique skill set through their ability to be resourceful to meet learning needs using data to inform instructional practices and make effective instructional changes. Additionally, we suggest using a framework (similar to the one discussed in this chapter) such as the Data Improvement Matrix for organizing a schoolwide leadership team to promote growth and progress within your school. Identifying a special educator as a school leader and data expert can assist in meeting the goals of schoolwide improvement plans, raise academic capacity, and foster confidence in other educators on their use of data within their classrooms and the school at large.

## How Special Educators and Data Can Foster Schoolwide Improvement

Effective data collection practices will assist school leadership teams in identifying areas of improvement within their school. Data experts can provide teams with appropriate data collection that matches an area the team is looking to improve. Once academic, social, or emotional data has been collected, special educators can examine the data to identify strengths, areas of improvements, obstacles, and trends. This step is crucial for school leadership teams because it provides a clear focus on the goals for improvement.

As noted in Chapter 4, special educators are highly equipped to increase student engagement, academic achievement, and foster positive behavioral support systems using individualized data systems. Teacher preparation programs are anchored in high-quality core competencies such as content specialization and pedagogy. Not unlike general educator preparation, special educator preparation programs aim to prime their teachers to evaluate and use high-leverage practices.

**STOP AND REFLECT**

1. What can I do to ensure we meet our annual growth goals?
2. How does my special education team influence my schoolwide decisions?

These practices are standards of high-quality teaching that inform the approaches special educators use to support students with diverse learning needs (McLeskey et al., 2017). These high-leverage practices for special educators include the identification and adaptation of appropriate instructional methods, the creation of individualized student-improvement plans, and the selection of suitable data-gathering measures to assist in positive outcomes, as well as evaluation of intervention effectiveness. The preparation of a special educator also includes collecting and analyzing individual and classroom data to inform if the practices, plans, and adaptations are effective for students. Furthermore, special education teacher preparation programs offer course content in collaboration, creating safe and effective environments, and confidentiality that are critical skills for leadership. Moreover, one of the cornerstones of special education preparation programs is the ability to assess contexts, academic or behavioral, and determine functions of student behavior's using multiple forms of data, in order to determine the next action step. Special educators are steeped in this practice through their preparation on Functional Behavioral Analysis (FBA). FBA is a process of identifying interventions that directly relate to the relationship between the unique characteristics of an individual's behavior and the function it serves them (Steege & Watson, 2009). Through this preparation, special educators use data and the problem-solving process to develop and implement interventions to promote student success. All teachers are required to collect data to inform their instruction, but special educator's preparation provide opportunities for accountability through data collection and capacity building for additional staff within the building (Fullan, 2005). General educators also analyze data for improvement of their classes. General educators use formative and standardized test to analyze class performance and create an action plan for future instruction, additional analysis is needed to create effective plans with explicit steps that are tied to goals (Bambrick-Santoyo, 2011). Designing explicit steps tied to a goal and collecting data lead to impactful change in instruction and student performance. The focus using data to design impactful instruction provides a basis for a focused problem solving that will provide clear, unbiased strengths and areas of improvement.

Special educators can often assist general educators with practices and data collection. Utilizing general educators for data collection is crucial to evaluate academic, social, and emotional student data. General educators and special educators alike can collaborate to create assessments that match concepts and skills being taught. These assessments provide teachers with specific data to make academic decisions for students based on their skill growth within a classroom setting. Similarly, classroom social and emotional behavior can provide descriptive understanding of student functioning within a classroom. The special educator can assist in creating data teams within grade levels or subject-specific content teams that evaluate student's academic, social, and behavioral growth within classroom settings by reviewing questions and skills through an overall analysis (Bambrick-Santoyo, 2011). Evaluating assessments develops a teacher's understanding of their classroom's learning and creates opportunities to review if a new practice should be utilized or if a practice has been effective. As a team, this can provide crucial guidance for reteaching, extension, or moving forward with an additional topic or skill. Special educators can collaborate and assist general educators to deeply analyze classroom assessment data to improve instruction and problem solve in order to develop and implement practices that promote a student's academic growth in a specific area. Analyzing classroom assessments can create the capacity and buy-in for general educators to review their own classroom's success on a consistent basis. These practices can provide classroom level data for leadership teams and administration to determine if intervention is needed across a grade level, content area, or schoolwide. Frequently measuring and improving instruction is essential to determine areas of strength and need at the student level, grade level, content level, or school level.

Schools use multiple sources of data such as, Multi-Tier Systems of Support (MTSS), IEP's, district wide surveys, district and national benchmark assessments, district's standardized test performance, and program evaluations to inform their practices and improve student outcomes. When schools fail to use data appropriately, or interventions do not adequately support student growth, student learning is hindered and teacher job satisfaction decreases. This can begin a tumultuous spiral for an administrator and a trench that is difficult to dig out from. Using data to better inform practices as well as using a key facilitator of that data is a best practice often underutilized. In this chapter, we introduce a Data Improvement Matrix, a protocol for recognizing current strengths and needs in your school's use of data and crafting a plan to improve outcomes for all students and staff. As such, special educators are poised to initiate and maintain the use of the Data Improvement Matrix within a school for schoolwide improvement. This matrix assists in the identification of the challenges schools face, as well as assists in the decision-making processes necessary for improvement.

## The Data Improvement Matrix

Even the highest performing schools have areas in which they can improve. For some, student academic achievement is critical; for others, it is students' behavior that requires improvement. Even in schools with well-developed systems, students with high-intensity needs require additional supports.

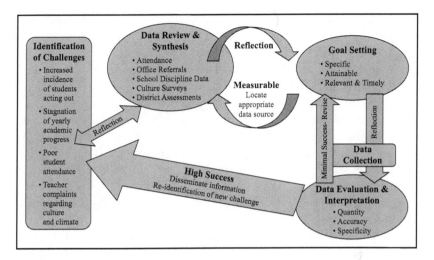

**Figure 3.1**  Data Improvement Matrix.

*Note. Rectangles denote schoolwide or subcommittee input; circles denote special education leadership. Arrows are moving pieces.*

In order to provide ongoing support with fidelity, individualized and targeted data collection systems are required. Regardless of which domain a school seeks to improve, it is likely that data will be a critical tool in measuring, reflecting, and analyzing progress. The Data Improvement Matrix, Figure 3.1, is a dynamic process in which a school administrator can use to engage their staff, elicit leadership from their special education data expert, and most importantly, foster improvement in their school.

## Identification of Challenges

Schoolwide leadership teams along with building administration are often tasked with creating improvement plans. In order to foster school improvement, specific areas of need must be identified. These areas vary between microlevel classroom challenges to more significant macrolevel school-based deficits.

---

### STOP AND REFLECT

1. What are the current methods for identifying our school's improvement needs?
2. Are we using a team-based approach when we identify challenges?

Administrators and leadership teams alike are able to identify these areas of improvement either by simple discussion or through top-down channels such as district school-performance report cards. These formal and informal means of knowledge inform the school community of their starting place for improvement. Identification of these challenges should not be seen as an anchor for reprimanding school staff, rather a platform to guide focus and base progress. Some examples of these challenges include increased discipline referrals, stagnation, or regression of academic progress, and poor camaraderie and climate amongst professionals. The first step in improving your school is to identify which challenge needs to be tackled to improve outcomes for students. Prioritizing school needs provides a vision and pathway to improvement. Using your school's leadership committee to identify this challenge is an excellent way to garner buy-in for school staff. Identification of these challenges should come from a source(s) of data.

## Application

Consider your school leadership team, and the distributive leadership models discussed in Chapter 2. Is your school leadership team using collaborative distribution, collective distribution, or coordinated distribution (see Table 2.2, Chapter 2)? To implement the school-improvement matrix, a team approach using distributed leadership is recommended. As the matrix follows a sequence, using the coordinated distribution model best aligns with this facet of school improvement. In the coordinated improvement model, work activities are performed in a particular order, for a shared goal, as they will be throughout the use of the school-improvement matrix. Another consideration includes the identification of the stakeholders in your leadership team, such as general educators, special educators, and support staff, as representation from each group may be required depending on school needs. Lastly, consider special educators at your school and how their experiences with data for a variety of purposes could be leveraged for leadership on this team. A team-planning guide (see Table 3.1) will assist your leadership team in assigning responsibilities, identifying schoolwide challenges, and the selecting appropriate data that corroborates those needs.

---

**STOP AND REFLECT**

1. Are there similarities between your school and Jankin Middle School?
2. What should the goal of the first leadership team meeting be?
3. How can the administrative team support the first meeting for success?

**Table 3.1** Team Planning Guide

| Meeting date | Purpose: Identification of challenges |
|---|---|

Leadership chair's name: _____

**Responsibilities:**

- Organize meeting dates and times.
- Facilitate sessions by supporting effective communication.
- Assess, interpret, and prioritize needs.
- Summarize each meeting's purpose and next steps.
- Data expert; synthesize findings.

| Team members: | Role and responsibilities: |
|---|---|
| 1. _____ | 1. Note taker |
| 2. _____ | 2. Time keeper |
| 3. _____ | 3. Technology assistance |
| 4. _____ | 4. _____ |
| 5. _____ | 5. _____ |
| 6. _____ | 6. _____ |
| 7. _____ | 7. _____ |
| 8. _____ | 8. _____ |

**Identification of school's challenges**

**(1) Host an open-ended discussion with all members about current status of school's needs and begin the brainstorm of challenges the school faces.**




**(2) Use the below grid to narrow challenges and identify data which supports the claim. End discussion by ranking each challenge by priority.**

| Description of challenge | Data that supports this priority | Ranking of importance |
|---|---|---|
| | | |
| | | |
| | | |

*(Continued)*

**Table 3.1** Team Planning Guide (*Continued*)

| Meeting date | Purpose: Identification of challenges |
|---|---|
| **(3) Identify next steps: What other data needs to be collected at the systems level, school level, and classroom level? Who is responsible for collecting that information?** | |
| <u>Systems level</u><br>• _____<br>• _____<br>• _____ | Person(s) responsible? |
| <u>School level</u><br>• _____<br>• _____<br>• _____ | |
| <u>Classroom level</u><br>• _____<br>• _____<br>• _____ | |

Throughout the remainder of the chapter, we will use a vignette as a guide for each step of the Data Improvement Matrix and provide good insight and application on the use of the Matrix in practice.

## Case Study – Part 1

Jankin Middle School has a population of 250 students with diverse ethnic and socioeconomic status. The school serves students in sixth, seventh, and eighth grades. On staff, there are three general education teachers per grade level as well as four special education teachers across the grades. Jankin Middle School also has support staff that includes teachers of the fine arts, physical education, a reading specialist, social worker as well as paraprofessionals, and counselor. At the end of the last academic year, budget cuts challenged the school, creating some tension between the school's administration, staff, and the support staff. Administrators just received the school's year-end performance report card, as regulated by the county, which was released in early July. It is now August and unfortunately, the school as a whole regressed in academic standing. The report card shows that 12% of the student population did not make adequate yearly progress on standardized assessments. Furthermore, as administration began to dive more deeply into the report card and schoolwide academic data, a significant slide was recognized for the entire sixth-grade team. During the course of conversations amongst the school administration, the topic of school discipline arose, which prompted the leadership to gather more data. Upon further review of the school behavior data (office discipline referrals, attendance, and climate surveys), administrators identified a trend. The school behavior data revealed increased incidence of disciplinary actions with consequences such as detentions and in-school suspensions across all grade levels. These concerns are among the top priority for administration upon entering the coming school year, and the principal has convened the leadership team for additional, paid school-improvement days. During the first leadership team meeting, administration introduces the Data Improvement Matrix (Figure 3.1) as well as the team-planning guide (Table 3.1). Administration has identified some of the school's challenges and sets the intention at the first leadership team meeting to dive deeper into uncovering challenges the school may have. Additionally, in the meeting, roles and responsibilities of all team members will be discussed, and next steps with a timeline will be laid out.

## Data Review and Synthesis

Once a challenge has been identified through either formal or informal means, the next step is to call on a special education data expert to assist in data review and synthesis. This second step allows for the data used in the identification of the school's challenge to be further examined. Also, this step allows teams to consider other possible sources of data that can be produced. For example, if a school's leadership team has identified through discussion and teacher survey that student discipline is a concern, the special education data expert would also want to review discipline referral data (detentions, suspensions, etc.), student behavior plans, as well as the school's positive behavior intervention and supports (PBIS) plan. Through this undertaking, the data expert would synthesize the information and summarize the findings. This dynamic process requires significant reflection as well as expertise in data interpretation, a task special educator do regularly through IEP preparation and student reevaluations. It is possible that over the course of reviewing the data, a new challenge might be uncovered; the actual root of the school's challenge. Using the previous example of school discipline, the data expert may uncover that the PBIS system is not being implemented with fidelity in all grade levels, thus causing higher referrals out of a particular classroom or grade, leading to the entire school's detention/suspension rates to increase. The school leadership team, as well as the data expert, and administration must be reflective throughout the entire improvement process. Progress is the responsibility of all parties.

## Application

At the end of your first leadership team meeting, you identified some of the school's challenges, ranked those difficulties, and discussed the need for more data collection from varied sources. A recommended next step is to introduce the use of a subcommittee, with your data expert as the chair. This subcommittee would gather and review all the data that reflects your school's needs and synthesize the meanings of that data. This subcommittee may be able to draw conclusions and links from the varied data sources to reflect a more accurate representation of the needs of your school. Then the subcommittee may review or collect additional data to ensure they are truly understanding the school's needs.

### Case Study – Part II

Ms. Golden, an experienced special educator at Jankin, has been nominated by her principal and leadership team to be the chairperson of this year's committee. Ms. Golden has a reputation for being incredibly detail oriented, and an excellent collaborator. The first meeting of the year was a success and it was determined that a subcommittee was needed to review the collected data; office discipline referrals, detention and suspension rates, the school climate survey, as well as last year's MTSS progress monitoring data. Together, with two general educators and a school social worker, the team notices a pattern across grade levels. After analyzing the data, they found that after the winter holiday break, progress monitoring slowed significantly, and office discipline referrals went up in all grade levels. This led them to wonder, what was happening at the school and classroom level in regard to school routines and discipline? The subcommittee began to investigate factors that could cause this change.

---

**STOP AND REFLECT**

What are some of Ms. Golden's key attributes that will make her a successful data expert and team leader?

---

## Reflection

Over the course of implementing the Data Improvement Matrix, teams should acknowledge that the process is dynamic with constant moving pieces. The reflection arrows are purposefully two-way. In order to make the most progress, multiple perspectives and thorough consideration of all possible outcomes are required particularly during the challenge identification and data collection stages of the improvement matrix.

## *Case Study – Part III*

After the first subcommittee meeting, Ms. Golden and her colleagues began to think more deeply about the return from the winter break. She wondered, are teachers forgetting to spend time reviewing classroom routines after the break, and is that causing students to act out more? The subcommittee needed to collect additional data to understand the school's needs. Ms. Golden began to have informal conversations with others in the school about their discipline practices after the holidays, and what emerged was that most people were very concerned with high-stakes testing preparation and spent little time on reviewing classroom management practices. Ms. Golden brought this new information back to her subcommittee to review and discuss the next steps based on the new data that was collected.

## *Goal Setting*

The exciting work of improving your school cannot exist without setting a relevant and attainable goal for improvement. Special educators are particularly adept at setting goals as one of the key components of their preparation as so much of their professional activity is goal writing for student IEP's and behavior intervention plans (BIP). Special educators use their expertise to write Specific, Measurable, Attainable, Relevant, and Timely (SMART) goals for every child they service (Doran, 1981). This skill transfers to creating school improvement goals. To ensure that a school improvement goal is effective, administrators, and leadership teams should craft goal statements that contain the same components as a good IEP and/or BIP goal. Your special education data expert is an asset in crafting these statements. As they will be familiar with the data used to identify the school's challenge, a specific and measurable goal will come more easily. The key in writing an effective goal is that the intervention is specific and that the measurement of the goal is clear, logical, and obtainable. Resources on SMART goal writing are available in Appendix B.

## *Case Study – Part IV*

Referring back to the data collected on school discipline referrals, the subcommittee can craft SMART goals, such as within the second semester, student office referrals will decrease by 25% according to office referral frequency data and student response to behavioral intervention data, with the use of behavior-management professional development targeted to each grade team, increased positive incentives for all classrooms (such as field trips, pep rallies, homework passes, or school dollars), and student-centered planning and BIPs for recurring offenders. The subcommittee would then be able to use the data to identify a challenge as well as determine how to measure the results within a specific timeframe. It also outlines a path for success and progress that the subcommittee can monitor through data collection.

## Application

Now that your leadership team and data collection subcommittee are established, a second meeting with the entire leadership team is in order. It is recommended that your data expert present the subcommittee's findings and facilitate a discussion regarding those findings. All stakeholders are necessary for this meeting as having the multiple perspectives that span grade levels and environments may provide more insight on the school's areas of need. By having all the stakeholders present a clear focus can be developed to meet the needs of the school. The outcome of this meeting is to reflect on the school's priorities from meeting one and set a SMART goal for the year's improvement. Use Table 3.2 to capture the essential components of this second school-improvement goal-setting meeting.

---

**STOP AND REFLECT**

How does having two goals impact each stakeholder group?

---

## Case Study – Part V

The Jankin's leadership team is excited to have a better understanding of the school's challenges. They decide that classroom management and school-wide positive behavioral supports begin strongly in the year; however, motivation to continue best practices wanes during the middle and end of the school year. After discussion on how to tackle this challenge, the team decides to write two goals. The primary goal is long term, and the secondary goal is more immediate and actionable. The Jankin's team wrote the following primary goal: By the end of this academic year, student academic progress will improve by four percentage points and school-wide discipline referrals will decrease respectively, with the use of more specific school and classroom-level positive behavioral supports such as reintroduction to routines once monthly through classroom meetings and grade-wide assemblies. Their secondary goal was: To improve school and classroom-wide practices on behavioral management, professional development will occur every other month, for 1 hour through workshops, train-the-trainer presentations, and online learning, with 90% staff attendance at each event, by the end of the year.

**Table 3.2**  Goal Setting Meeting

| Meeting date | | Purpose: Goal setting | |
|---|---|---|---|
| Attendance | | | |
| 1. _____ | | 5. _____ | |
| 2. _____ | | 6. _____ | |
| 3. _____ | | 7. _____ | |
| 4. _____ | | 8. _____ | |
| **Description of challenge** | **Data that supports this priority** | | **Hypothesized underlying cause** |
| | | | |
| **SMART goal setting** | | | |
| **Targeted challenge**<br>Area your school most needs improvement | | | |
| **Specific intervention**<br>Intervention you will use to improve school outcomes | | | |
| **Measurement tool**<br>Data you will use to measure success | | | |
| **Time bound**<br>By when you expect this goal to be completed | | | |
| **Final primary goal statement** | | | |
| **Secondary goal** | | | |

## Intervention and Data Collection

The intervention your school chooses is one that is a direct reflection of the goal set by your leadership team and special education data expert. The intervention may be specific to a classroom, entire grade, or to the entire school. The expectations for who, how, and when the intervention will be delivered should be clearly outlined. Furthermore, the type of data that will be collected throughout the use of your particular intervention should also have distinctly defined parameters. It may be helpful to refer back to the goal statement as the intervention(s) are being conducted to ensure that adequate progress is being made. For more information and resources on data collection, see Appendix B.

---

**STOP AND REFLECT**

1. What type of data will be collected?
2. Does data collection occur during the intervention, after the intervention, or both?
3. Who will collect the data?

---

Your special education data expert will act as a guide throughout the intervention delivery and data collection phases of school improvement. A special educators' preparation relies heavily on addressing the needs of students and pairing effective strategies to promote growth. Special educators are creative and resourceful and are wonderful problem solvers. These key skills are critical when thinking about delivering an intervention. Furthermore, as special educators are trained to teach all learners, delivery of professional development to other staff members is a skill well suited to these teachers. For more information on the expertise of special educator and their ability to deliver programming to other educators, see Chapter 5. Additionally, to learn more about a special educator's ability to creatively solve problem, see Chapter 6.

### Application

At your last meeting, the leadership team decided on two goals for your school's improvement over the next year. These goals should include an actionable intervention. Your data expert will assist in making sure accurate records are collected throughout the intervention process to ensure that you are meeting school goals. This may include training and delegating other members of the leadership team on methods of data collection.

### Case Study – Part VI

Jankin school is excited about the goals they have set for the coming year. The leadership team crafted a schedule for informal collegial classroom observations for every other month to observe teachers and their classroom management practices. In order to have successful observations, the leadership crafted a checklist for observations and practice on one another to become more comfortable with the process of taking data as well as being observed by peers. For the secondary goal, Ms. Golden has delegated taking attendance data for each of the school's professional development activities to different members of leadership team. A timeline was created to review the goals and data collected. Additionally, the leadership team met to assess the school's progress towards their goals during second semester.

## Data Interpretation and Evaluation

Once data is collected on the effectiveness of your chosen intervention, that data must be analyzed and often triangulated with other sources of data. Again, your special educator is an expert at using formal and informal data to determine the effectiveness and progress of a goal. A special education student's IEP is based primarily off continuous data collection and analysis, thus who more apt to analyze school improvement data? Furthermore, special educators have a good grasp of the learning what is happening 'on the ground.' Often, special educators move in and out of multiple classrooms and can provide perspectives of many different classrooms. This ability to see good teaching and know the practices of the school as whole positions a special educator to know how effectively interventions are received within classrooms. Once the data is triangulated, formal analysis can be completed. This analysis will determine if your target for improvement has been achieved. If so, congratulations! You have successfully implemented the school improvement matrix and have positively impacted the growth of young minds. If not, congratulations! Using the data, you can trace exactly where the breakdown occurred and you are one step closer to school improvement. With the assistance of your team, you are able to revisit the goal and identify whether you would like to try to a different intervention or perhaps you have uncovered a deeper truth about the challenge that needs to be attended to before you can continue.

## Application

Throughout the school year, you have crafted a schedule of meetings with your leadership team. At each meeting, you establish a routine of revisiting the learning challenges, data, and goals your team has set. Additionally, when new data becomes available you ask your data expert to review the data with your team and continue to have discussion regarding the school's progress. This continuous schedule of meetings creates accountability and supports follow through with your plan and goal(s).

## Case Study – Part VII

Ms. Golden and the leadership team have done an excellent job staying motivated throughout the school year. The team was able to conduct many classroom observations and the school as a community became increasingly more comfortable with having data collected at the classroom level in order to improve instruction. Throughout the year, there were professional development sessions that occurred; however, it was difficult to track all the individual learning that was occurring throughout the year. At the end of the school year, before state data was announced, the leadership team was able to end the year with a celebration for the school as office discipline referrals went down and the school met its secondary goal.

## Re-Matrix

As mentioned previously, school improvement is never-ending. Once improvement has been made, take the opportunity to celebrate with your school community. Disseminate the information and give praise individually and widely; everyone has done their share to improve outcomes for students and staff. Furthermore, your special educator has been instrumental in assisting the growth of the school as a whole. Begin using the matrix again to continue the progress and improvement of your school.

### Application

Celebrate the milestones your school has accomplished and take a moment to reflect on the progress. Set meeting dates for over the summer to continue to use the leadership team to its full capacity and begin the work for the following year's improvement. Use the Summary Page (Table 3.3) to reflect on process.

## Case Study – Part VIII

The leadership team is thrilled to have worked so hard and seen success using the matrix this year. They planned a schoolwide celebration for the end of the year and crafted a schedule to meet once over the summer to review the state's data. Their focus with the leadership team and data collection helped the school stay focused on their goals and enact change. Overall, they plan to continue the use of the leadership team, data expert, and School-Improvement Matrix.

**Table 3.3** Data Improvement Matrix Summary Page

| 1. Identification of school's challenges | | |
|---|---|---|
| Ranking | Description of challenge | Data that supports this priority |
| | | |
| | | |
| | | |

| 2. Goal setting | |
|---|---|
| **Targeted challenge** Area your school most needs improvement. | |
| **Specific intervention** Intervention you will use to improve school outcomes. | |
| **Measurement tool** Data you will use to measure success. | |
| **Time bound** By when you expect this goal to be completed. | |
| **Final goal statement** | |

| 3. Data evaluation and interpretation | | |
|---|---|---|
| Data source | Interpretation | ✓ Met goal |
| | | |
| | | |
| | | |

(*Continued*)

**Table 3.3**  Data Improvement Matrix Summary Page (*Continued*)

| 4. Summary and information dissemination | |
|---|---|
| **Summary:** | |
| | |
| **How will information be disseminated?** | **Who will disseminate?** |
| | |
| **5. Next steps** | |
| | |

## Using a Special Educator as a Data Coach

Eliciting progress within a school can be daunting work. The familiar eye-roll from an educator who is averse to change and is particularly vocal about their reservations about the new policy or procedure can be difficult to manage. When these new policies require educators to collect data, the grumbling at the staff meeting becomes audible. Often, this grumbling is misunderstood; most educators are tasked with accomplishing so much within a given day that adding another 'to do' causes feelings of being over-whelmed and may also induce anxiety. In particular, when mandates are top-down, and not seen as collaborative efforts, educators are less likely to be excited to make change.

Many educators are unfamiliar with the most current and best practices of data collection and this unfamiliarity causes the resistance to use data as a tool for school-wide improvement. Special educators are not data super-heroes; they just have the preparation needed to know how to intertwine data collection seamlessly with instruction. This familiarity and comfort with the different methods of data use and collection positions your special education staff perfectly to assist your more reserved teachers. A data coach is a special educator within your school community who has strong data collection skills as well as strong leadership qualities and is able to teach their colleagues how to seamlessly integrate data collection within their everyday teaching routines. Even if your school has a process in which school improvement occurs, a data coach is a simple, and effective method to improve data usage within your school.

Implementing the use of a data coach within your school has the following benefits:

- Promotes special educator leadership
- Data collection becomes approachable and increases schoolwide buy-in
- Builds a culture of community and collaboration
- Provides cost-effective, within-house professional development

While using a data coach as part of the **Data Improvement Matrix** is beneficial, a data coach within your school can also assist teachers within the building on a more regular basis; thus providing mentorship in a practical, targeted, and student-centered way. Teachers who are seeking to improve the quality of their instruction and student-learning outcomes will seek out the data coach to improve their professional practice. If the opportunity is not afforded to them, they have limited means to improve their data practices and they will continue to find data collection off-putting. The groans will become louder and louder with each new improvement plan and growth target.

Data coaches can be embedded into your school as the chair of a leadership team as mentioned previously in this chapter. However, a data coach could also be used throughout grade-level team meetings or in content specific subcommittees. Schools often have subcommittees that are responsible for evaluating current practices and the curriculum with regard to content such as a math or social studies team. A data coach on each of these teams would offer a wealth of knowledge and could provide the team with some valuable insight on how the current practices are affecting student outcomes. Data coaches in this capacity could focus on specific areas of growth as needed and identified by your school.

## Summary

As you have read throughout the chapter, special educators are instrumental in assisting your school's improvement through data. Their skills of implementing and collecting different sources of data, as well as analyzing and interpreting the information positions special educators to be high-quality leaders and change agents in your school. Special educators are prepared and skilled at using data to implement interventions and measure progress, an essential factor for school improvement. The use of the **Data Improvement Matrix** facilitates and streamlines the process in which to use your special education leader as well as foster growth within your school. To assist in gaining teacher capacity, a special educator can also serve as data coach within your school. Data coaches facilitate professional development and leverage evidenced-based practices to improve student outcomes, as well as a culture of collaboration within your school.

## Next Steps

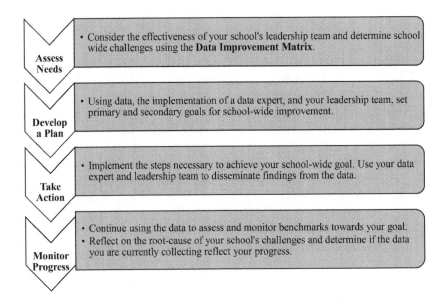

- **Assess Needs** · Consider the effectiveness of your school's leadership team and determine school wide challenges using the **Data Improvement Matrix**.
- **Develop a Plan** · Using data, the implementation of a data expert, and your leadership team, set primary and secondary goals for school-wide improvement.
- **Take Action** · Implement the steps necessary to achieve your school-wide goal. Use your data expert and leadership team to disseminate findings from the data.
- **Monitor Progress** · Continue using the data to assess and monitor benchmarks towards your goal. · Reflect on the root-cause of your school's challenges and determine if the data you are currently collecting reflect your progress.

## References

American Association of School Administrators. (2002). *Using data to improve schools: What's working.* [Report]. American Association of School Administrators. https://aasa.org/uploadedFiles/Policy_and_Advocacy/files/UsingDataToImproveSchools.pdf

Bambrick-Santoyo, P. (2010). *Driven by data: A practical guide to improve instruction.* John Wiley & Sons.

Doran, G. T. (1981). There's a S.M.A.R.T. way to write management's goals and objectives. *Management Review, 70*(11), 35–36.

Fullan, M. (2005). *Leadership & sustainability: System thinkers in action.* Thousand Oaks: Corwin Press.

McLeskey, J., Barringer, M-D., Billingsley, B., Brownell, M., Jackson, D., Kennedy, M., Lewis, T., Maheady, L., Rodriguez, J., Scheeler, M. C., Winn, J., & Ziegler, D. (2017). *High-leverage practices in special education.* Council for Exceptional Children & CEEDAR Center.

Morrison, J. (2008). Why teachers must be data experts. *Educational Leadership*, *66*(4), 4–8.

New, J. (2016). *Building a data-driven education system in the United States*. Center for Data Innovation. Retrieved from http://www2.datainnovation.org/2016-data-driven-education.pdf

Steege, M., & Watson, T. S. (2009). *Conducting school-based functional behavioral assessments: A Practitioners Guide* (2nd ed.). Guilford Press.

# 4

# DATA-BASED INDIVIDUALIZATION

## Geraldo Tobon, James Hanley, and Kasandra Posey

Several students are not making appropriate progress at Hamilton Elementary. Most of these students receive special education services to meet their individual academic and/or behavioral needs. General education teachers are referring the other few students who are not making adequate academic and/or behavioral progress for special education services.

| Administrator's perspective | Special educator's perspective |
|---|---|
| I am responsible for making sure the school as a whole is making adequate growth. Therefore, I feel the pressure for all subgroups of students, including those with disabilities, to make growth. I am receiving pressure from general education teachers who want their students to receive extra services. Our school has adopted a wide array of academic and behavioral interventions. In addition, students with IEPs are receiving additional supports and services. Why are they not making adequate growth? | The only way for students with disabilities to make progress is to take an individualized approach. We should be using student-level data to tailor the interventions we have to meet our students' academic and behavioral needs. This is a process that requires lots of individualized attention, professional collaboration, and resources. Growth might be small at times for some students and various adaptations to an intervention may be needed before a successful approach is found. |

**Key Points:**

- Understand that **data-based individualization (DBI)** is a method for intensifying and individualizing interventions for students with persistent and challenging learning and/or behavioral needs.
- Explain how to use **DBI**, an adaptive process of individualizing interventions for student's specific academic and behavioral needs, **using frequent data collection.**
- Identify ways of **tapping into special educators' key unique skills** to successfully implement DBI at your school.
- **Plan** ahead for potential challenges that might arise when implementing DBI school-wide.

Academic achievement and success for *all* students is what good administrators strive for, but there are often a few students whose progress is not what it should be. It is not uncommon for schools to have students who do not make adequate academic and/or behavioral progress despite receiving high-quality universal instruction, in addition to evidence-based secondary interventions. The lack of progress these students experience is, in most cases, attributed to their severe and persistent learning and/or behavioral needs. It is estimated that 1.5 million students in the United States have severe and persistent learning and/or behavioral needs that have a negative impact on their academic progress and post-school outcomes (National Center on Intensive Intervention [NCII], 2013). These students require intensive interventions tailored to their specific learning and/or behavioral needs. The question that comes to mind for school administrators and teachers working with these students is, 'How do I provide individualized interventions that allow our lowest achieving students to make adequate progress and, in turn, improve our school-wide data?' The answer to this question has been something that educational professionals have struggled to answer for many years.

To ensure success for students who make little or no progress with universal instruction and evidence-based secondary interventions, processes and systems need to be in place to meet the needs of students with intensive learning and/or behavioral profiles. Two systems many school districts have implemented are Response to Intervention (RTI) and the more comprehensive Multi-Tiered Systems of Support (MTSS). Both RTI and MTSS rely on the use of data at all levels of the problem-solving process, starting with universal screening and continuous progress monitoring across tiered supports. MTSS differs from RTI in that it also emphasizes the importance of school culture, teacher professional development and collaboration, and family and community engagement (Cunningham, n.d.).

> **STOP AND REFLECT**
>
> 1. How does your school meet the needs of students not making progress with evidence-based secondary interventions?
> 2. Are teachers' specific knowledge and skills used to help these students and the other staff members that work with them?

MTSS also focuses on student social-emotional well-being in order to support student's behavioral and academic needs. Within an MTSS/RTI system, all students receive high-quality Tier I, universal instruction. Those not making progress with Tier I are placed in Tier II which consists of providing students with an evidence-based secondary intervention in the area they are struggling in. Students not responding to the additional support are then placed in Tier III and, in addition to receiving high-quality universal instruction and a secondary evidence-based intervention, are also provided with intensive individualized interventions.

Administrators are charged with ensuring the smooth implementation of RTI or MTSS to see to the success of students struggling in school. However, RTI and MTSS are not always implemented with consistency across schools or even classrooms. The hallmark components of an effective RTI/MTSS system are assessment, interventions, and evaluation. All three are critical in identifying which students need support, providing students with the correct intervention, and evaluating the effectiveness of the interventions provided. Without a foundation in the above components, schools will struggle with supporting all students. Further, the lack of clarity on how to best support students requiring more intensive support make it even more challenging for schools to meet the needs of our most vulnerable students. Schools are also responsible for ensuring students with disabilities make adequate academic and behavioral progress. This is done by ensuring special education programs and RTI/MTSS work side by side to prevent unnecessary referrals to special education and by ensuring students with disabilities receive services by implementing individualized education programs (IEPs). Despite intensive individualized intervention being the hallmark of special education, it is not always effectively implemented (Vaughn & Wanzek, 2014). Our most vulnerable students fall further behind because of the lack of knowledge on how to individualize interventions.

One powerful method for improving outcomes for students with disabilities who do not make adequate academic and behavioral progress, and for strengthening tiered systems already in place, is data-based individualization (DBI) (NCII, 2013). DBI is a method of ensuring students with the most challenging learning and/or behavioral receive the targeted supports needed to make adequate progress. DBI is not to be confused with data-based instruction. DBI involves tailoring evidence-based interventions using individual, student-level data as a guide. In contrast to DBI, data-based instruction is the use of *classroom*-wide data to tailor whole group instruction whereas DBI uses *individual* student data to drive the selection of *individual* student interventions. The main difference between DBI and data-based instruction is the focus on the individual rather than the collective. DBI is an effective framework to ensure that students are receiving individualized instruction based on their unique learning profile rather than using a classroom-wide learning profile.

Implementing DBI not only leads to improvements in school-wide data by targeting the most challenging students, but it also leads to a more inclusive school in the process (Fuchs et al., 2010; Gresham, 2004; Wanzek & Vaughn, 2009). By finding ways of helping our students with the most severe and/or persistent learning and/or behavioral needs, including students with disabilities, make progress, school-wide growth targets can be met with greater frequency. Many times, administrators seek to improve outcomes for all students but unknowingly only target students with mild to moderate academic and/or behavioral needs.

In the process of targeting only students with limited needs in an attempt to improve school-wide outcomes, students with severe and persistent academic and/or behavioral needs are inadvertently excluded and left behind. For example, the implementation of MTSS has shown success for students with limited difficulties in behavior and/or academics. However, there continues to be challenges in effectively addressing the needs of students with more severe needs who are not responding to Tier II interventions (Braun et al., 2018). Although this type of exclusion is not visible, it has real consequences in the form of not doing what we can to help close the achievement gap that exists between students with disabilities and their peers. DBI becomes a way to not only improve outcomes but also a mechanism for ensuring inclusion of students with disabilities with severe needs in school-wide improvement efforts. Schools have a valuable resource at their disposal to assist in rolling out a school-wide DBI initiative, the special educator.

## What is DBI?

DBI involves the continuous collection and analysis of individual student data to inform the tailoring of evidence-based interventions to meet the individual academic and/or behavioral needs of students (NCII, 2013). DBI is not an intervention that can be grabbed from a shelf and implemented by following a script or specific curriculum. Rather, it is a process that allows for the identification of how to adapt evidence-based interventions, those interventions demonstrated to work across multiple experimental research

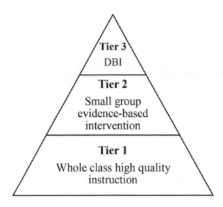

**Figure 4.1** Tiered Model.

studies, to meet the specific academic and/or behavioral needs of a student. For example, when a student is not making behavioral progress with a Tier II intervention such as check-in/check-out, intensification and individualization of that intervention are required.

In an RTI or MTSS model, DBI fits within the third tier of support (see Figure 4.1). For some schools, this is the last attempt at providing struggling students with supports before referring students to special education. For other schools, Tier III is special education for students identified as having a disability that impacts their learning. In either scenario, students in this tier demonstrate a lack of progress with both high-quality Tier I instruction and evidence-based Tier II small group interventions. In Tier III, students receive intensive and individualized interventions based on their area(s) of need while continuing to receive Tier I and Tier II instruction.

**STOP AND REFLECT**

1. What approach do special education teachers take at you school when providing academic instruction and behavioral supports?
2. Do you believe you have a strong special education program at your school?

Just like all students, those with disabilities should be receiving high-quality instruction that produces positive academic and behavioral outcomes. DBI, then, is a method that makes special education special. It is instruction that allows students with disabilities to meet their IEP goals and make overall educational progress in the content areas. In addition to academic progress, DBI supports students with behavior needs to allow them access to the academic content. These instruction and supports are based on individual needs. Unfortunately, some students often receive less than adequate education when placed in special education. This lack of quality education is due to a lack of individual attention, lack of time engaged in rich academic practice, and lack of quality of instruction, which contributes to increased gaps in achievement and poor postsecondary outcomes when compared to their peers without disabilities (Newman et al., 2011; Vaughn & Wanzek, 2014). DBI can be used as a foundation to a high-quality special education program and a strong Tier III for students struggling who are not in special education.

## Before Implementing DBI

The process of implementing DBI begins when a student is not responding to an evidence-based Tier II intervention, which is typically a ready-made, standardized intervention program that includes a script and student materials (e.g., Academy of MATH, Reading Recovery) or an evidence-based instructional practice (e.g., check-in/check-out and repeated readings). However, several considerations need to be kept in mind before beginning the DBI process. It is important that before the DBI process begins, students are receiving interventions that match their areas of need. Your school should have available Tier II interventions for the content areas and behavior. If your school is lacking this, then before attempting DBI, your school's MTSS team or intervention team should select a number of interventions to implement. For a list of evidence-based Tier II interventions see Appendix B for more resources (e.g., National Center on Intensive Interventions and What Works Clearinghouse website).

It is crucial that Tier II interventions be delivered with fidelity as intended by the developer of the intervention if it is a program or as recommended if it is an instructional practice. This is important because it might not be the students' learning needs that are the issue, but the lack of adequate implementation of the intervention. To avoid this confusion, the use of an intervention fidelity checklist is useful. Most intervention programs come with a fidelity checklist; Table 4.1 is an example of a general fidelity checklist. An intervention implemented with high levels of fidelity has components implemented 80% or more of the time. The purpose of fidelity is to ensure that the implementation of the intervention is in accordance to the steps outlined by the intervention developer. One way administrators can develop the use of fidelity checks at their schools is by having teachers outline the core components of an intervention and rate their fidelity following implementation. Another approach is to have another staff member observe implementation and complete the fidelity checklist at a determined frequency (e.g., weekly

**Table 4.1** Fidelity Checklist

| Skill | Always | Sometimes | Rarely |
|---|---|---|---|
| Follows script/directions as indicated by developer. | | | |
| Maintains good pace as indicated by developer (e.g., gets through all parts in 30 min). | | | |
| Provides intervention with consistency as indicated by developer (e.g., provides interventions three times a week). | | | |
| Follows assessment protocol as indicated by developer. | | | |
| Actively engages all students. | | | |
| Effectively manages behavior and avoids interruptions. | | | |

Place a checkmark in the appropriate box based on the following scale:

Always = Demonstrates skill 80% or more of the time.

Sometimes = Demonstrates skill 25–80% or more of the time.

Rarely = Demonstrates skill less than 25% of the time.

An intervention followed with fidelity will yield all skills as demonstrated always.

and monthly). Analyzing fidelity data on a regular basis during MTSS or other applicable team meeting will ensure that interventions are being delivered as intended.

Consistent progress monitoring is another crucial component that needs to be in place before implementing DBI. As noted in Chapter 4, progress monitoring is a process of collecting data on the targeted academic skill or behavior and determining whether the student is making progress or not. Progress monitoring allows educators to know in real time how students are performing. By looking at immediate gains in the targeted skill or behavior, it allows educators to determine what to target next which will lead in more global measures of achievement. Through progress monitoring it will become apparent whether a student is responding to an intervention or not. If progress monitoring is not in place, it will be difficult to tell how well a student is responding to an intervention and whether the DBI process should be started. For resources relating to progress monitoring see Appendix B.

Lastly, before beginning the DBI process, members of the IEP team, MTSS team, or similar team need to ask themselves whether the issue lies within a mismatch of intervention. It is possible that the intervention chosen does not match the needs of the student. For example, if a student is receiving structured breaks as a behavior intervention and has not demonstrated a change in disruptive behavior, it could be that the intervention does not match the function of the student's behavior. The student could be acting in a disruptive way because he is seeking attention. Therefore, structured breaks, which are interventions most useful for escape behaviors, will have little effect in changing the student's behavior. Similarly, with an academic skill, a child having difficulties with decoding will not benefit from an intervention with a heavy emphasis on comprehension.

---

**STOP AND REFLECT**

1. What areas of assigning and providing interventions to struggling students is your school good at?
2. What areas does your school need work in?

---

## Implementing DBI

Once progress monitoring indicates that the student is not responding to the evidence-based Tier II intervention, despite matching the student's area of need and that the intervention is delivered with fidelity, the intervention needs to be implemented with more intensity. The following three methods represent options to intensify the intervention: (a) Increase the amount of time the student receives the intervention, (b) change the grouping of students to ensure more opportunities for the student to receive instructional feedback, and (c) ensure instruction is delivered consistently across contexts (Vaughn et al., 2012). Increase in learning time includes frequency (e.g., amount of days per week a student receives intervention), duration (e.g., the number of minutes a session), and length of an intervention (e.g., the number of weeks an intervention takes place). Grouping involves the reduction in the number of students in the intervention group. Intensifying intervention through instructional delivery involves being more explicit and systematic with instruction. Being more explicit requires that the teacher overtly teach skills and concepts through clear steps. Being more systematic involves breaking down any skill or concept into smaller chunks of learning. See Table 4.2 for examples of intensifying interventions and items administrators should consider regarding intensifying interventions.

### *Case Study 1 – Part I*

Ms. Gomez is a first-grade general education teacher and her student, Sarah is struggling in reading. She has been receiving the school's Tier II reading intervention program which provides intervention on decoding,

**Table 4.2** Examples of Ways of Intensifying Interventions

| Ways of intensifying intervention | Example | Administrator consideration |
|---|---|---|
| Increase in learning time | Andrea is not making progress with the reading intervention that is provided three times a week. The teacher has noted she quickly forgets the skill or concept taught previously, therefore, she decided to intensify the intervention by providing Andrea with 5 days of intervention. | It is simple to extend intervention length by providing more weeks of intervention. It is more challenging to increase the duration or frequency of intervention. This might involve being flexible and creative with scheduling and staff organization. Adding a block specifically for interventions can help in extending interventions provided during scheduled content area time. Training paraprofessional staff in the intervention can assist in finding staff that will extend intervention time. |
| Grouping | Juan is receiving math intervention with six other students; however, he is not making progress. Reducing the group size to three allowed the teacher to provide him with more attention and he was able to demonstrate growth. | Having smaller groups will involve having more groups. This in turn will require more staff to deliver interventions for the additional groups. Again, paraprofessional staff can be trained in delivering intervention. Further, other capable teachers with flexibility in their schedules can be trained in delivering interventions (e.g., the art teacher). |
| Instructional delivery | Daniel is making little progress with math intervention on problem solving. His teacher notices that he becomes easily confused with the problem-solving steps of the intervention. In order to assist Daniel, she broke down the problem steps further and provided more explicit instruction by modeling and thinking aloud as she provided instruction. | Creating professional learning communities and integrating this information during professional development can assist staff in how to deliver explicit and systematic instruction. |

comprehension, fluency, and vocabulary. Ms. Gomez notes that she has made very slow progress based on her progress monitoring data (running records). Sarah does not participate much during intervention and Ms. Gomez feels this is contributing to her lack of progress. She is concerned that she is falling behind and decides to try using the DBI method to intensify and individualize the Tier II intervention to meet Sarah's unique learning needs. She begins intensifying the intervention by reducing the size of the group that Sarah is in during the reading instruction because of Sarah's lack of participation. Ms. Gomez decides that a grouping of three students, instead of five, will allow her to give Sarah more attention and opportunities for immediate feedback, individualized attention/instruction, and error correction. The increase in intensity might be enough for Sarah to begin responding to the intervention.

If intensifying the intervention fails to improve students' performance, then it is necessary to adapt the intervention to meet the student's unique learning and/or behavior needs. Diagnostic assessments, which include research-validated assessments, such as a decoding skills screener or an error analysis of student work samples, are used to determine gaps in students' skills or understanding. The results obtained should than be used as the basis for adaptation of the intervention. Using the data gathered from progress monitoring and the diagnostic assessments, the teacher should set a realistic goal to work toward.

### Case Study 1 – Part II

Ms. Gomez notices that she is not making progress with the intensified reading intervention, so she decides to give her a phonics decoding skills survey because her running records indicated she has trouble reading accurately. The decoding skills survey suggests that Sarah is making mistakes reading words that contain long vowel patterns with two or more syllables. Ms. Gomez adds additional instruction and practice on reading words with long vowel patterns, specifically those with two or more syllables, as an adaptation and sets a realistic goal for Sarah. Based on the data, Ms. Gomez believes that Sarah is capable of reading text that contains more than a dozen words with long vowel patterns with 80% accuracy and full comprehension of the text.

The remainder of the DBI process is then guided by the continued use of data. After intensification and adaptations are made to the Tier II intervention, progress monitoring should be continued to determine the effectiveness of the newly adapted intensified intervention toward meeting the students' goal(s). If progress monitoring indicates that the student is not making progress, then diagnostic data should be collected to determine further adaptations should be made to meet the student's academic or behavior needs. This iterative process of data collection, analysis, and intervention adaptation continues until the student has shown sufficient progress. Figure 4.2 shows a visualization of the DBI process.

### Case Study 1 – Part III

Ms. Gomez notes that Sarah has made little progress with the newly adapted intervention. She decides to analyze her running records further to determine where she is struggling. She notices that Sarah struggles with remembering what she has read. She then adapts the intervention by adding additional opportunities for comprehension strategy instruction around self-monitoring. After several weeks of this newly adapted intensive Tier II

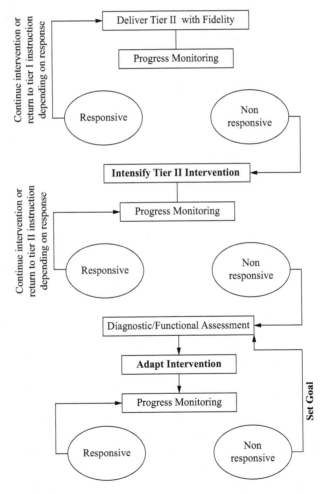

**Figure 4.2** DBI Model.

intervention, Sarah has demonstrated growth in reading by improving her decoding and comprehension skills.

## Implementing DBI for Behavior

The DBI process can also help in improving success in behavior. The following case of Rob demonstrates how the DBI process can help intensify and individualize behavior interventions.

### *Case Study 2 – Part I*

Rob is a fourth-grade student who is receiving Tier II intervention to meet his behavior needs. Rob struggles with focusing and getting attention appropriately. He is currently on a check-in/check-out system that includes teacher rating of behavior on school expectations at predetermined times throughout the day. The in-class ratings represent points earned and Rob can redeem the points for a reward. Rob's special educator, Mr. Colby, notes that the intervention has been unsuccessful in decreasing the frequency of Rob's disruptive behaviors. To meet Rob's behavioral needs, Mr. Colby decides to intensify the intervention by increasing the number of check-ins throughout the day and providing Rob with an opportunity to earn a reward for meeting expectations both in the morning and afternoon.

After several weeks of the intensified intervention, Rob demonstrates little behavioral progress. Following the next step in the DBI process, Mr. Colby conducts a functional assessment (FBA) and reviews Rob's behavior rating sheets to determine how to individualize the intervention further. The purpose of conducting an FBA is to determine the function of Rob's behavior. An FBA involved collecting additional data, including detailed observational data and interviews with the student and school staff, that will help pinpoint the function of a behavior. After completing the FBA and reviewing Rob's point sheet, Mr. Colby notes that most of Rob's behaviors are occurring during language arts time and they appear to serve a function of escape. He comes to the conclusion after noting in his observations that the behavior occurs immediately after an assignment is given during language arts. In addition, an interview with Rob's general education teacher gives further evidence to the function of the behavior. Rob's general education teacher states that Rob finds the reading material difficult and typically experiences frustration. Rob's general education teacher noted that he is doing poorly in class and Rob complained on multiple occasions that the work is too hard.

Knowing that Rob is struggling with his behavior because he finds the reading difficult and determining the function of his behavior, Mr. Colby makes several adaptations to the Tier II interventions in place. To address the academic concerns, Mr. Colby collaborates with Rob's general education teacher on what is going to be taught. This way, Mr. Colby can discuss what is going to be covered in class with Rob during the midday check-in and provide Rob with a brief overview of the skills to prepare him for language arts. Further, Mr. Colby and Rob's general education teacher collaborate on how to provide Rob structured breaks when Rob becomes frustrated throughout class time. They teach Rob how to recognize when he is becoming frustrated and ask for one of a limited amount of breaks he can take. During these timed breaks, Rob can engage in a preferred activity to help reduce his frustration before returning to his classwork. Mr. Colby discusses the new changes with Rob, and they set a goal of receiving 80% of his points on his behavior sheet for a week straight within 6 weeks. After 6 weeks of the adapted intervention, Rob has made progress and has met his goal.

## Essential Skills for Making DBI Work

To effectively roll out DBI, a leader with key skills are needed, including someone who is collaborative, competent with data, an expert in instruction, an individual with high levels of adaptive expertise, and an effective advocate for student needs. As a school administrator, you want to maximize your resources in effecting change and increasing student outcomes. Special education teachers represent an important resource at the administrators' disposal who can lead efforts in DBI because of their distinctive experiences and training.

---

**STOP AND REFLECT**

Think of effective special education teachers at your school. What unique skills do you believe they possess?

---

Working with other educational professionals has become a necessity in education, and this holds true for DBI. In a DBI model, general education teachers, special educators, interventionists, or other professionals providing intensive individualized intervention cannot work in isolation. The DBI process requires the knowledge of all teachers working with the particular student with challenging and persistent learning and/or behavior needs. As noted in Chapter 2, special educators are no strangers to collaboration. IEP meetings represent only one of the many opportunities special educators have in collaborating and refining their collaborative skills. They must work alongside their general education counterparts, related service providers, community agencies, and parents year-round to ensure the success of their students in school as well as to ensure a smooth transition post school.

Special educators can bring together everyone's expertise in implementing DBI to meet the needs of students, including the general education teacher's knowledge of implementing Tier II interventions.

The cornerstone of the DBI process is the continued collection and use of individual student data. Without strong data collection, DBI will fail to meet the needs of students with severe leaning and/or behavior challenges. Therefore, a strong foundation in data collection and analysis is essential. Special educators work at providing instruction and setting attainable goals based on the analysis of a wide range of data. The data that special educators consider when working with individual students and creating individualized education plans include standardized tests, classroom assessments, diagnostic tests, and individual progress monitoring data. Not only are special educators well versed in administering and analyzing individual student data, they consider school-wide and classroom-wide data when working with their students as well (see Chapter 3). Considering today's push for accountability for all students, it is essential that teachers be able to analyze classroom and school-wide data. However, special educators have the advantage of being experts in the use of individual data and instructional adaptation. They can focus on individual students needs and respond appropriately.

Implementing DBI requires that teachers deliver Tier II intervention with adaptations effectively through high-quality instruction. Without this crucial component, the use of data and collaboration will not be fruitful. The actual delivery of an individualized and intensified intervention is through high-quality instruction. It is no longer following a script but continually adapting instruction to meet the student's needs to ensure results, something special educators have a lot of experience with. Special educators can provide instruction based on individual student needs and individual goals all while considering the behavioral needs students may have in an effective and efficient way. They plan accommodations and modifications to meet individual student needs and they provide accommodations or modifications during a lesson on the spot to reach all students. Special educators' instructional expertise is a result of their characteristic as expert learners. They actively seek new knowledge to fill gaps in their existing knowledge base.

Adaptive expertise is the ability to tap into one's knowledge base and be able to innovate in a novel situation efficiently and effectively. Refer to Chapter 6 for more details on adaptive expertise. High levels of adaptive expertise are key in the DBI process considering that students who require intensive individualized intervention are those who are not able to be reached through standard means. Teachers implementing intensive, individualized supports using a DBI model need to efficiently use data, tap into their knowledge base of what works for students, and innovate in order to tailor the Tier II intervention to meet the student's unique learning and/ or behavior needs. Special educators encounter novel situations in greater proportion to general educators, it's the nature of the job. Through years of experience with novel situations and constant reflection, special educators acquire high levels of adaptive expertise. When implemented, DBI, requires teachers to constantly adapt and innovate based on their student's responses to the interventions which can be determined based on the data.

Students with disabilities who require intensive and individualized interventions are our most vulnerable students and therefore require adults who will advocate for them. Advocates need to question and challenge current practices and structures that are not working to meet the needs of this population of students. Without effective advocacy, the sustainability of a school-wide DBI initiative is not likely. Refer to Chapter 8 for more information on advocacy. Because DBI is an iterative process, constant adaptations and revisions are necessary in order for students to make progress. The iterative nature of the DBI process has the potential of becoming an initiative that is abandoned because it does not provide quick results. DBI is a powerful tool that can ensure results if followed consistently and with patience. Advocates for children with the most significant and persistent learning and/or behavior needs are an essential component to the successful implementation of DBI school-wide. Special educators' unique role has given them experience to develop the necessary skills and disposition of an efficacious advocate. They know their students and the services they need and deserve and persevere through challenges to make sure their students receive them.

---

**STOP AND REFLECT**

Consider the unique skills special education teachers have. How can you leverage special education teachers as leaders of DBI in your school?

---

## Challenges to Implementing DBI

Implementing a school-wide DBI system will not be without its obstacles. Keeping potential roadblocks and challenges in mind before rolling out DBI school-wide will mitigate their potential effects. Three major challenges in the implementation of DBI include teacher buy-in, knowledge around implementing individualized supports, and teacher concerns with not having adequate content knowledge that will support individualized instruction. Special educators can assist in minimizing these challenges.

In light of the push for increased accountability and testing, DBI might seem like an additional duty that teachers will have to do, in turn reducing the amount of buy-in from teachers. Buy-in refers to teachers' willingness, interest, and openness to be part of a new initiative. To mitigate the potential lack of buy-in from teachers, Schumacher et al. (2017) suggest that one or two eager teachers be chosen to pilot DBI before rolling it out school-wide. The obvious candidates for a pilot program are special educators. Student gains from a small-scale implementation of DBI has the inherent possibility of increasing other teachers' interest in the DBI process. Further, it can assist in identifying kinks with the process and areas in which teachers might need additional training. This can in turn inform the professional development opportunities that can be provided to teachers.

To address the lack of knowledge around providing individualized intervention a strong and continual focus on multi-tiered support should be included throughout the DBI professional development provided to teachers. An expert teacher who is knowledgeable on tiered supports as well as intensive and individualized interventions should be identified to provide insight on how to provide learning opportunities for teachers. Again, special educators have experience and knowledge in this area.

Lastly, teachers' concerns around having sufficient content knowledge to provide individualized interventions across content areas are a barrier that can be tackled through ongoing professional development. One suggestion is incorporating best teaching practices and specific instructional strategies around the areas of concern for teachers with continuous professional development that will help lessen that anxiety, and increase teacher confidence and assist in teacher buy-in. Special educators have plenty of experience with using many kinds of teaching practices and instructional strategies for students with the most challenging and persistent learning and/or behavior needs and this knowledge and experience should be tapped into when creating professional development for DBI. Special educators are expert learners and will go out of their way to make sure they have a deep understanding of instructional practices that other teachers may lack.

## Leveraging Special Educator Expertise

DBI is an effective approach for meeting the needs of students who have the most challenging and persistent learning and/or behavioral needs. Fortunately, special educators receive training on each aspect of the DBI process including progress monitoring, evidence-based practice selection, and adaptation of components to enhance the match between student need and intervention components. As such, special education expertise can be leveraged to support broader adoption of DBI and improved outcomes for students with disabilities. That is, special educators are prepared to collaborate, collect and analyze data, adapt instruction, and advocate for student needs. Allowing special educators to take more active roles in the development of DBI school-wide can harness their unique skills to ensure successful implementation. Team leaders, creating PD, and coaching other teachers are just a few roles special educators can take when implementing the DBI

**Table 4.3** Roles to Encourage Special Educator Teacher Leadership

| Role | Definition |
| --- | --- |
| DBI team leader | Special educators can lead a team dedicated to referring students to the DBI process and monitoring their progress. Their expertise with collaboration and analyzing data makes them prime candidates. |
| Professional development developer | To ensure a smooth role out of DBI, all staff members involved educating students with severe and persistent learning and/or behavior needs would need to be provided with professional development around the DBI process. Special educators' knowledge of intensive and individualize support can support the development of effective PD. |
| DBI coach | In addition to quality PD, staff members involved in the DBI process will need coaching on how to implement and feedback on how well they are implementing. Since special educators have expertise with providing individualized support based on data, they can provide teachers valuable feedback on their practice. |

process in a school-wide setting. See Table 4.3 for a quick overview of roles special educators can take on to support DBI school-wide.

To ensure the successful implementation of DBI, the creation of a DBI team should be considered. The function of a DBI team is to identify students needing intensive individualized intervention, monitor student progress, ensure fidelity of implementation, adapt and intensify interventions based on data analysis, and support teachers in providing intensive interventions. For administrators of schools with small number of students and staff, consider integrating DBI into one of your already existing teams (e.g., MTSS team, School Improvement Team, etc.). The obvious leader for such a team is the special educator. As mentioned above, special educators possess collaborative skills that can assist in collectively working together with various professionals when determining how to intensify and adapt interventions for struggling students.

Another possible way of leveraging the expertise of special educators is in the form of having them build or provide professional development. The successful implementation of a school-wide DBI will depend highly on the competence and capacity of the staff implementing the DBI process. A way of informing school staff on the DBI process is by providing professional development along with build-in time for coaching. Effective professional development should be relevant, continuous, and provide opportunities for practice. Because special educators are already part of the staff and work closely with a wide array of educational professionals, they will be able to make professional development relevant and feel worthwhile. In addition, special educators' expertise with creating education plans for individual students can help them create a long-term professional development series that does not end with just one surface-level workshop. Special educators, by the very nature of their jobs, have worked with countless students who exhibit the most severe and persistent learning and/or behavior challenges. This experience can inform the creation of case studies in which the DBI method could be applied during professional development sessions.

The successful implementation of DBI in schools will require constant reflection and feedback. Special educators' adaptive expertise and collaborative skills make them excellent candidates to help teachers starting the DBI process for the first time by providing coaching. Their data expertise will allow them to work with teachers in identifying the skills that need to be targeted which will inform the adaptation. In addition, they can use their instructional expertise to coach teachers on effective practices and behavior strategies that align to the specific learning or behavior needs of students. Lastly, special educators' experience with novel situations and how to tackle those situations efficiently in innovative ways make them the perfect DBI coach candidate.

There is no doubt that special educators have a unique set of abilities that can be leveraged in multiple ways to support implementation of a DBI process school-wide. Despite being equipped with unique skills and training, special educators need to be supported in this endeavor. As mentioned above, special educators make effective coaches, team leaders, and professional development creators. Special educators should be provided with additional time to put toward their efforts in those areas in order to be successful. This will require administrators to be creative when scheduling and allowing special educators flexibility as well. If possible, reducing potential special educator leader's caseloads will help them focus their attention on ensuring a smooth and successful school-wide implementation of DBI which will in turn improve outcomes for students across the school. Reducing caseloads may not be feasible in some schools. In these cases, providing more planning, or integrating this role within current structures, like existing professional learning communities, or grade-level teams, could make the work less daunting. Lastly, valuing special educator leader's efforts by providing recognition and allowing them autonomy over the work they are doing will help in supporting them. A less authoritative and more collaborative, distributive approach should be used with trying to leverage special educators' unique abilities. Failing to do so can make special educators feel as though they have been given one more task to complete.

## Summary

DBI is a powerful method of providing our most vulnerable students with supports that will allow them to make academic and/or behavior progress. Successfully implementing DBI throughout the school will not only improve school-level data and provide a more inclusive environment, but it will also strengthen MTSS by improving knowledge of effective tiered interventions that will work for all students. DBI can help a school make leaps and bounds by ensuring *all* students make progress; however, the success of DBI will largely depend on strong systems to support implementation across the school. It is a great framework to compliment a schools' already existing tiered supports, but without expert leaders that demonstrate key skills and understandings, these efforts may fall short. Special educators' skills in collaboration, data use, teaching, advocacy, and high levels of adaptive expertise should be utilized as they are all crucial skills necessary to a successful DBI system.

## Next Steps

**Assess Needs**

- Reflect on current systems and structures in place to identify struggling students, supporting those students, and monitoring progress. What is working and what can be improved?
- Identify a reliable and highly effective special educator or teachers who can serve as leader(s) for DBI implementation and identify other key professionals that can be part of a DBI team.

**Develop a Plan**

- Determine whether your staff has an adequate amount of Tier II interventions and are knowledgeable on how to use them as well as implementing them with fidelity. Plan for professional development based on staff need.
- Determine structures, systems, and procedures needed to identify struggling students, how interventions will be assigned, how progress monitoring data will be reviewed, and when to intensify and adapt interventions.

**Take Action**

- Develop a DBI team, or incorporate DBI procedures into an existing team, that will oversee the DBI process.
- Establish a system for identifying and documenting which students will require DBI. Be specific (e.g., students need to demonstrate lack of progress with 6 weeks of Tier II intervention).
- Identify professional development that can increase staff knowledge on intensive interventions.

**Monitor Progress**

- With the help of special education teacher leaders and DBI team identify teachers' needs in order to create an effective professional development series.

# References

Braun, G., Kumm, S., Brown, C., Walte, S., Hughes, M. T., & Maggin, D. M. (2018). Living in tier 2: Educators' perceptions of MTSS in urban schools. *International Journal of Inclusive Education.* DOI: 10.1080/13603116.2018.1511758

Cunningham, B. (n.d.). Understood. Retrieved November 15, 2019, from https://www. understood.org/en/school-learning/special-services/rti/whats-the-difference-between-rti-and-mtss

Fuchs, D., Fuchs, L. S., & Stecker, P. M. (2010). The "blurring" of special education in a new continuum of general education placements and services. *Exceptional Children, 76*(3), 301–323. https://doi.org/10.1177/001440291007600304

Gresham, F. (2004). Current status and future direction of school-based behavioral interventions. *School Psychology Review, 33*(3), 326–343.

National Center on Intensive Intervention (NCII). (2013). *Data-based individualization: A framework for intensive intervention.* Office of Special Education, U.S. Department of Education.

Newman L., Wagner, M., Knokey, A.-M., Marder, C., Nagel, K., Shaver, D., Wei, X., with Cameto, R., Contreras. E., Furgurson, K., Greene, S., & Schwarting, M. (2011). *The post-high school outcomes of youth with disabilities up to 8 years after high school. A report from the National Longitudinal Transition Study-2 (NLTS2)* (NCSER 2011-3005). SRI International. https://nlts2.sri.com/reports/2011_09_02/nlts2_report_2011_09_02_complete.pdf

Schumacher, R. F., Zumeta Edmonds, R., & Arden, S. V. (2017). Examining implementation of intensive intervention in mathematics. *Learning Disabilities Research and Practice, 32*(3), 189–199. https://doi.org/10.1111/ldrp.12141

Vaughn, S., & Wanzek, J. (2014). Intensive interventions in reading for students with reading disabilities: Meaningful impacts. *Learning Disabilities Research and Practice, 29*(2), 46–53. https://doi.org/10.1111/ldrp.12031

Vaughn, S., Wanzek, J., Murray, C. S., & Roberts, G. (2012). *Intensive intervention for students struggling in reading and mathematics: A practice guide.* RMC Research Corporation, Center on Instruction. https://files.eric.ed.gov/fulltext/ED531907.pdf

Wanzek, J., & Vaughn, S. (2009). Students demonstrating persistent low response to reading intervention: Three case studies. *Learning Disabilities Research & Practice, 24*(3), 151–163. https://doi.org/10.1111/j.1540-5826.2009.00289.x

# 5

# INSTRUCTIONAL EXPERTISE

## Courtney Lynn Barcus and Bryan Moles

Students have just completed a mathematics bell ringer reviewing fractions that have been taught over the last week. During the 'do-now' activity, both the general education and special education teachers actively monitor the students while they work. Together they announce a timeline for pacing toward completion and gave a clear goal for students to work toward. The general education teacher circulates reviewing student work on the left side of the room while the special education teacher circulates on the right side. Seating arrangements were at random with mixed ability. As the 'do-now' activity wrapped up, the educators met to strategize next steps toward the day's upcoming lesson based on the observed work.

| General education expert teacher | Special education expert teacher |
|---|---|
| Wow! About 80% of my students displayed excellent understanding on the 'do now.' There is a small group of students who have some misconceptions about the last problem, but we are still working on that skill anyway, so they have time to get it. Today I will make sure to get students to use the math vocabulary numerator, denominator, and | I need to circle back with Sonya, John, and Arman to make sure that they use their fractions strips with today's lesson. They missed the problem on the 'do now' but were doing great with similar problems yesterday during our small group rotations. Mari and David came in from lunch at frustration level already. I think they need some time to calm down and reengage, I will check their |

*(Continued)*

fraction bar. It seems like they are mixing up those terms. The ones who really didn't get it both have IEPs. I wonder if the special education teacher can pull them for a small group today so that she can teach yesterday's lesson again because they really need to get that before they can move on. I have extra copies of the worksheet we used, so I need to be sure to send those with her today. work again on the first or second problem to see if they are able to refocus. Kieana seems to be missing the conceptual understanding. While the class gets their homework written down, I will sit with her and show her two other students' work that used visuals to answer the problems. Those visuals show the connection between the conceptual and the numeric representation.

**Key Points:**

- **Redefine** the qualities and skills associated with an expert practitioner to include **strategic, knowledgeable, and motivated**.
- **Capitalize on expert special educators** who have specialized training in learner development and difference, a broad range of pedagogical tools, and individualized planning, instruction, response to data, use of instructional tools, and implementation of student supports.
- Leverage special educators' instructional expertise to **support individual teachers, grade-level teams, and schoolwide systems, to create a more inclusive professional community**.

In the above scenario, we see that both educators fall into similar paths of thinking. They both consider the content for the course, necessary adjustments, and maintain a clear eye for student success. These thoughts are not uncommon for any educator as they circulate during student work time. Where we begin to see these two experts diverge is in the way that they consider their next steps.

The general educator is focused on the instructional plan and the overarching goals of the grade level. You might imagine the path that the general educator has mapped out as a long, wide river covering various topics and skills, with the majority of the class flowing along together as a group on a large boat. This path may have some turns and shifts, but overall the class stays together. Bow or aft, students are still bound to the boat as the general education teacher navigates it down the river, even if they need to linger longer in one area or on one skill to establish mastery.

Comparatively, we see the special educator focuses in on each student's functioning, needs, and next steps on an individualized basis. Returning to the river analogy, there is a stark contrast to the single boat of the general education teacher. The journey still holds the long, wide river in its scope; however, the special educator has arranged for several alternate methods of transportation as well as divergent courses for different students. It might include narrow and meandering streams, bridges to cross, and mountains to climb. The starting point of the journey may have been different for many of the travelers, but the goal is that all students, whether general education or special education, are able to make progress toward the goal in a way that works for them.

The true synergy here is in the general educator and special educator using their varied perspectives and knowledge in order to advance the success of the class as a whole. When the two maps are overlaid and utilized in conjunction, all students benefit from the complex travel systems that result.

In order for these two very different instructional plans to be able to work in harmony, a school must be set up to equally value and advance the development of both general education and special education teachers. For this, school administrators must have a clear understanding of the types of expertise and the associated knowledge that teachers bring to the instructional environment. This chapter outlines these types of knowledge in order to redefine our current view of what makes an expert instructor. The resulting definition of *expert instructor* will allow for a more equal representation of general and special educators at the schoolwide level. This chapter also foregrounds the areas of expertise that special educators hold and offers administrators suggestions to leverage these skills to support a more effective and inclusive schoolwide community.

## Why Special Educators as Instructional Leaders?

School leaders are responsible for developing a team of educators that will work together to form a strong and effective school community. The team must not only have specialists in charting the course and navigating the boat, but must also include those skilled at charting new territory, finding alternate paths, and building bridges when necessary. Finding the right combination of educators can be a complicated job for administrators. They must form a balanced and complementary group that has extensive knowledge, can drive increases in student achievement, and – increasingly – collaborate with a range of stakeholders. To balance their school's unique needs, administrators will often search for teachers with high levels of expertise in areas or subjects that align to their school vision or instructional priorities.

As the context of public education continues to evolve for students with disabilities and their teachers, expectations about inclusivity and collaboration have risen based on federal legislation in the United States such as the *Every Student Succeeds Act* (ESSA) and the *Individuals with Disabilities Education Act* (IDEA). In this way, we see the need for more collaborative teaching partnerships where general and special educators work together to provide the instructional support for all students in a classroom. When special educators who are explicitly trained in these collaborative practices are utilized in leadership roles, they have the opportunity to share their instructional expertise beyond their co-teaching assignments. To learn more about the benefits of and methods for collaboration, see Chapter 7 on collaboration. The mandates put in place in the United States by *No Child Left Behind* (NCLB) have driven an increased focus on using data to improve accountability, as well as higher expectations for content and technological knowledge (Benedict et al., 2014; Lindstrom, 2017; Sindelar et al., 2014). As demands change and as implementation becomes increasingly more nuanced, having a special education leader who is well versed in these regulations, and has the skills needed to organize and analyze data sets, is of the utmost importance. To learn more about structures and strategies for data use, see Chapter 3 on using data.

To further complicate things, current research trends show administrators being tasked with leading professional growth for the school. As a result, they must also be able to provide a professionally stimulating environment for the teachers that they employ (Bettini et al., 2017; Hoppey & McLeskey, 2013). In order to do this, administrators must meet teachers where they are, provide individualized supports and strategies for professional growth, and continuously encourage current and innovative practices. This type of professional support closely resembles the instructional plans that special educators design for individual students. Thus, their thinking and planning processes could be utilized at the schoolwide level in order to improve the professional practice of all teachers.

## Connecting Expertise and Knowledge

Expertise and knowledge are intrinsically linked. To understand the ways that knowledge leads to expertise, we must first understand the various types of knowledge and how they are displayed by educators. There are three types of knowledge that a teacher might possess: declarative, procedural, and conditional. These can all be acquired through exposure, experience, and/or education.

Declarative knowledge, or 'knowing that,' (Alexander, 1992) tends to include the more domain or subject-specific knowledge. For teachers this is the knowledge of content that is necessary for them to understand the material that they are expected to teach. Before math teachers can teach math, they must first be able to engage in the actual process of solving math problems, think and reason about the math problems, and access tools necessary to complete them. Often, general education content teachers are strong in declarative knowledge.

Procedural knowledge, or 'knowing how,' (Alexander, 1992) tends to include the pedagogical steps associated with education. This includes not only knowledge of what the steps are, but why they are that way, and the ability to navigate the steps effectively and efficiently. For teachers, this is the understanding of *how* to actually teach the math that they know how to do. This typically includes devising multiple methods for completing one problem, as well as a variety of strategies for teaching the methods. Often, special educators have a great strength in this procedural knowledge.

Finally, conditional knowledge, or 'knowing when and where,' (Alexander, 1992) considers that education as an enterprise operates within social constructs, and the interactions within those constructs create unique situations that require the teacher to make decisions based on the context of the particular moment. In these situations, the special educator must take action through analyzing the situation, considering strategies that have worked in the past, and then applying a revised set of steps to address the need. This adaptation and expert problem solving describes the adaptive expertise that special educators also possess. To learn more about conditional knowledge and how it supports the development of adaptive expertise, see Chapter 6 on adaptive expertise.

While declarative and procedural knowledge are clearly two very different forms of knowledge, there is interdependency between them (Shulman, 1986). As teachers increase their content knowledge, they must simultaneously increase their processes, and structures for organizing those new understandings. In addition, in order to be able to use this content knowledge, they must develop new techniques and strategies for implementing it, thereby increasing their pedagogical knowledge.

The process of knowledge acquisition does not happen in isolation. When considering how knowledge connects to expertise, we must also consider the skills necessary to acquire that knowledge. Ultimately, the process that one goes through in developing content or pedagogical knowledge and the ability to implement that knowledge could be summarized as an expertise in learning (Meyer et al., 2014).

## Expert Learning

Experts commonly are conceived as those who have amassed a large amount of knowledge in a particular subject and have reached an 'absolute' state of effective operation in that area (Chi, 2006). It is often assumed that these 'absolute' experts have been in their field for a long time, have acquired a significant amount of knowledge through years of experience, and have undergone the necessary credentialing and learning required to be named an expert. Simply put, expertise is a 'rite of passage,' and is not reflective of the skills needed to meet current educational needs. Harkening back to the river analogy, this expert would be a person who can easily navigate the long, wide version of the river with the expected boat over the expected bridges to arrive at the expected destination.

Considering the shifts that we see in the field of education, this 'absolute' definition of expertise is out of date and must be reconsidered. By shifting our thinking to a more 'relative' consideration we see that expertise is more of a continuum and that our participation in certain activities affords us a level of expertise in those areas (Chi, 2006). Expertise and level of skill are intertwined, and as skill level increases in one particular activity, expertise is achieved within that activity (Kotzee, 2014). In this conception, we accept that while the long, wide river is one option for the trip, there may be other routes that can be taken. These routes may require smaller boats, or even that we build our own bridge. In this conception, we know that knowledge is dynamic and changes over time. When we consider expertise as a more 'relative' opportunity, we shift our focus to how one builds skill and improves performance in a certain area, and therefore how one becomes an expert at learning.

According to the Universal Design for Learning (UDL) (CAST, 2018), the ultimate goal of instruction is to develop expert learners. In turn, having the characteristics of an expert learner is a critical component to becoming an expert teacher, team member, or leader. In their unique role, special educators are tasked with meeting a variety of student needs within a variety of subject areas. As a result, special educators typically develop expertise in multiple content areas, as well as in the pedagogical strategies for addressing individual student needs.

Figure 5.1 shows how the definition of expertise can be redefined and shows the characteristics that these experts hold, as well as the skills that are associated. The skills represented within the Revised Conception will earn respect from colleagues, rather than receiving it as a 'rite of passage.' Administrators can leverage these important skills not only to increase student achievement and inclusivity within the classroom, but also at the

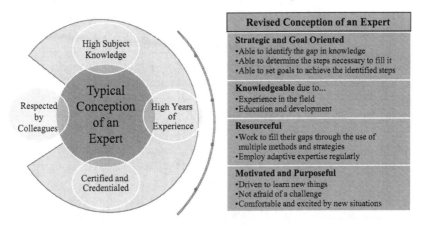

**Figure 5.1** Revised Conception of an Expert Teacher.

schoolwide level. The next section will name how special educators exemplify these skills of expert learning within the instructional context.

---

**STOP AND REFLECT**

Think about this new definition of expertise…
   Expert learners are

- Strategic and goal oriented
- Knowledgeable and resourceful
- Motivated and purposeful
   1. Which of these expert characteristics do I possess?
   2. How do I model these characteristics for my staff and students?
   3. Who in my building is also an expert based on these characteristics?

---

## The Instructional Impact of a Special Educator

In every classroom, there is a large group of students who exhibit average performance, consistently falling within the middle of the pack. Many teachers are able to make progress with this group of students. The challenge lies with the students who fall outside of this middle group, whether currently performing above average or below average. Many teachers, even expert ones, can struggle to achieve consistent growth with these groups. Students that are achieving ahead of the rest of the class face the constant challenge of maintaining above average levels of achievement. Without the proper support, rigorous instruction, and high expectations, we often see them begin to slide back toward the middle of the pack. Students who fall below the average group may do so for any number of reasons such as ineffective teachers, school absence, and learning difficulty. Many may narrowly miss the qualifications for special education (e.g., learning disabilities and mild cognitive impairment), but this does not mean that they do not need, or would not benefit from, the support a special educator can bring. Students in both of these groups may require a more *individualized* educational experience.

Studies demonstrate that effective general education teachers often have thorough content knowledge that meet the needs of the larger group of same-aged peers (Shulman, 1986; Zigmond & Kloo, 2017). That is, they are effective at teaching to those students who perform at the average level within the grade level. General educators use their extensive content knowledge to plan and deliver instruction that is expertly tied to grade-level standards and provides a strong foundation for those achievers in the classroom who are approximately performing at the grade-level average.

Special educators, on the other hand, possess a depth of understanding of different learning styles and needs, the vertical alignment of standards and skills, and the pedagogical methodology to reach a variety of student learning profiles. They receive specialized training and have a job description that allows them to apply these skills with an *individual student view* to effectively address the needs of those students on both sides of the average pack – those that perform above the grade level and those that perform below (Sindelar et al., 2014; Stough & Palmer, 2003). The very individualized nature of their role, however, makes it difficult for special educators to be experts in all areas of their profession. They are likely to encounter moments when a student's need or a content area is unfamiliar. In order to meet their students' needs, special educators must identify their own gaps in knowledge, set goals, seek new learning, track their own growth, and ultimately create new understandings around the previously unfamiliar area. In these ways, special educators often exemplify the skills of expert learning.

The next three sections will describe how special educators can exemplify the characteristics of an expert learner (strategic and goal oriented, knowledgeable and resourceful, and purposeful and motivated) (CAST, 2018), how these characteristics are connected to clear instructional actions, and how special educators employ these characteristics with an individual student view in order to gain a broader impact in the classroom and directly support students who perform outside of average. In each section, readers will have the opportunity to consider a school-based scenario where the skills listed above are employed to effect higher performance at the schoolwide level.

### *Strategic and Goal Oriented*

The entirety of any special educators' instructional experience is based on the individualized nature of their instruction. While many are internally driven to set and achieve their own professional goals, they are also held accountable for their work through the constant analysis of student Individual Education Plan (IEP) goals. It is the special educator's responsibility to set goals based on data and grade-level standards, establish a plan toward the goals, collect data regularly to track progress, and adjust the plan as necessary. The experiences that the special educator gains through this process are an invaluable resource for administrators. The goal-oriented nature of their role allows them to be comfortable with analyzing data, developing manageable goals, implementing interventions, making adaptations to those interventions, and regularly tracking progress toward these goals. To learn more about how special educators employ data practices see Chapter 3.

To effectively track progress toward any goals that are set, special educators take into account students' most effective form of expression. The UDL guidelines (see Appendix B) indicate that multiple options for knowledge expression should be provided to students and that teachers should employ supports for those who are still developing in skills and should employ alternatives for those who are ready for more independence (CAST, 2018). This idea directly connects with the premise of special education. Students with explicit learning challenges often benefit from being provided multiple options for expressing their knowledge. For example, a student with dyslexia may still be working toward writing a five-paragraph response to a debate question, but may be able to engage verbally in that debate with fluency. Special educators consider the format of knowledge expression based on the diverse needs of the students on their caseload as well as the variety that is represented within the whole class. As a result, they are comfortable providing a variety of strategies and tools for students' expression of knowledge.

---

### STOP AND REFLECT

Imagine tapping into the natural tendencies of goal-oriented individuals to guide school wide level work.

How could their experience with goal setting and tracking be used to support schoolwide goals, data tracking, and academic growth?

### Consider this ...

Your school has identified a trend that students are lacking investment on the quarterly benchmark assessment. Teachers are frustrated that students don't seem to take the assessments seriously. Your special educator suggests using a goal tracking template where students graph their own growth on the assessment and are able to see their progress over time. After implementing this for two quarters teachers share a marked difference in student investment and focus during testing days. On testing day, students exit the assessment smiling and exclaim, 'I passed my goal!'

---

### *Knowledgeable and Resourceful*

Special educators rarely identify as a 'grade-level' teacher. Instead, they are often in placements where they serve a wide range of grade levels and frequently address multiple content areas daily. Because of this, special educators are generally very resourceful, and once they know their teaching assignment will pursue professional development and personal research around that area.

In addition, they are often tasked with unpacking grade-level standards to scaffold students' learning. For example, a special educator may be assigned as a mathematics co-teacher in a sixth-grade general education classroom with several students performing significantly below grade level. These students might be performing anywhere from the second-grade level to the fifth-grade level, yet are receiving sixth-grade-level instruction. Special educators might look at students' IEP goals and the grade-level standards to determine pathways to move the student closer to grade level. They may strategically look at standards across grade levels and determine how they build on each other in order to teach the key thinking and practices that will increase student performance. As a result, the special educator often develops a clear understanding of the vertical alignment of standards across grade levels (see Appendix B), building their 'declarative knowledge,' or content knowledge.

---

### STOP AND REFLECT

Imagine how innate resourcefulness could broaden the perspective at the schoolwide level...

How might resourcefulness bolster problem-solving around tight budgets, gaps in coverage on the school schedule, or other various schoolwide needs?

### Consider this ...

After a schoolwide data analysis deep dive, you notice that the majority of students are showing strong growth, but those students who had previously scored above average are now falling in the middle of the pack. Your special educator asks about the use of flexible grouping and application of vertical alignment of objectives across grade levels. Teachers indicate that they know little about the expectations in the next grade level. Your school implements a vertical alignment planning meeting once a month to support teachers in better understanding the grade-level expectations above and below the grade level that they teach.

---

### *Motivated and Purposeful*

Special education teaching roles are based off of the student population and the exhibited need within. As the population changes, assignments also change. Considering this, it might be expected that a special educator would struggle to maintain motivation through these evolving role expectations. As expert learners, however, many special educators are highly motivated by new learning opportunities and take great satisfaction from overcoming frustrations and challenging situations. It is because they are aware of how they learn that they are able to regulate and advocate for their own needs within these changing conditions.

Not only are special educators motivated in their own professional growth, but they are also able teach motivation to both their students and their colleagues. On a daily basis, special educators break down larger metacognitive processes into smaller action steps that can be taught to others. Often these processes are not considered within the standards of a grade-level plan. They might include executive functioning, social interaction, or, in this case, how to maintain motivation when faced with a challenge. They can break down the idea of motivation into the discrete behaviors, mindsets, and organizational structures that are necessary for one to stay motivated. For example, for a student struggling with motivation, a special educator might use a variety of interest inventories (see Appendix B) to identify a source of motivation, cocreate a series of self-talk statements the student can use when motivation feels low, and employ organizational structures to check and monitor motivation throughout the school day. These instructional actions will begin to build the metacognitive processes to teach motivation.

---

### STOP AND REFLECT

Imagine you leverage this high level of motivation to support schoolwide engagement ...

How might this motivated teacher be able to help others overcome frustration and increase engagement?

### Consider this ...

You have a flexible professional development day approaching. You administer an anonymous survey to all teachers and find they would like new classroom management ideas because their old strategies feel stale and they have some 'frequent flyers' who they are feeling frustrated with. You reach out to your most successful special educator who is regularly called upon to respond to challenging behavior scenarios and ask if she would be comfortable leading a session. She agrees and asks for a more specific outcome for her session. After the two of you review the survey data, you co-plan two objectives for the staff professional development and determine how you will assess staff response. Your special educator plans the session and in an exit survey, teachers' responses indicate that they are highly satisfied and feel positive about meeting students' behavioral needs.

---

## Benefits of Special Education Instructional Experts on the School Community

In order to be successful, it is important that special educators possess the characteristics of expert learners and know how to implement strategies in the classroom as instructional experts. The benefits to individual students and classrooms are many, and include higher levels of student engagement, understanding, and expression of learning (Meyer et al., 2014). The benefits can also extend to the school level. Administrators should emphasize these characteristics. By doing this, they may reap the following benefits:

- Building a culture of goal setting with both teachers and students will support increased student achievement.
- Broadening each teacher's perspective will allow the analysis of all data points rather than just the median or mean, thereby increasing academic achievement.
- Increasing student engagement will decrease negative behaviors.
- An individual student view will increase the shared responsibility across ALL school professionals.

Improved student behavior, increased student achievement, and a shared accountability among staff will all support a more inclusive and collaborative schoolwide culture (Cook et al., 2019). In order to realize the aforementioned benefits and fully leverage special educators as instructional experts, it is critical that they be fully integrated into all instructional decisions within the school. Full integration includes the equal involvement of special education and general education teachers in all relevant decisions that are made within a school, regarding the curriculum, resources, assessments, and instructional methods that are used.

With equal participation from general and special educators, schools will be able to achieve balance in the decision-making process. This collaboration allows for decisions to be made that support learners at all levels and of all abilities (Billingsley & Banks, 2019), with general educators driving the decision-making process to support the majority of the student body, and special educators identifying strategic shifts to reach learners beyond those in the average range. Full integration in instructional planning decisions allows leaders to leverage the unique characteristics of special educators as instructional experts, resulting in a stronger school culture. The next section will detail various ways to achieve these results.

---

### STOP AND REFLECT

1. How inclusive is my school community?
2. Are my special educators fully integrated into the instructional planning and decision-making process within the school?

Are they included in the following ways …

- in all educator professional development sessions?
- in schoolwide leadership teams?
- in grade-level teams?
- in Professional Learning Communities?
- in coaching positions?

## Leveraging Your Experts

As expert learners and instructors, special educators should be used as a model of best practice not only within the classroom, but also within the larger context. This can be done at three different levels: one-on-one teacher pairings, team structures, and schoolwide initiatives. The following sections detail various roles and responsibilities in which these educators can be employed to leverage their expertise.

### *One-on-One Teacher Pairings*

As detailed in Chapter 7, special educators are highly skilled collaborators. A major component of their job is to be able to network with and coordinate a team of people that will work together to support the student in question. These effective collaboration skills make them a great candidate for pairing with other educators in various roles. Some examples of these roles are listed in Table 5.1.

In making personnel decisions for their school, leaders must take into account the skill sets that each educator brings to the table. They must look at the varying levels of preparation that teachers receive, the years and experience with content, the grade level needs of the school, and teachers' credentials (Stough & Palmer, 2003). They must ultimately work to create partnerships that balance strengths and areas for growth. When making these decisions, it can be all too easy to begin the process by placing general educators in their respective roles and finding them a grade-level partner with whom to work. Special educators are then placed depending on the special education population needs without an eye toward the balance of expertise within each classroom and the respective co-teachers. Instead, special educators' skills should be foregrounded to make strategic pairings between educators for mentoring, coaching, or co-teaching partnerships.

### *Team Structures*

Just as they can be leveraged to support individual teachers, special educators make for highly effective team leaders as well. Grade-level teams, Professional Learning Communities (PLCs), Instructional Leadership Teams (ILTs), Multi-Tiered Systems of Support (MTSS), and School Improvement Teams (SIP) all require a leader who has high levels of instructional capacity. The function of each of these teams is to identify, analyze, and strategize around problems that arise within an instructional context. A leader of these teams must be able to effectively set goals, be resourceful in finding solutions, and persevere toward solving them, all while holding a clear focus on instruction. The expert learning characteristics that special educators hold make them perfect candidates for these leadership roles.

**Table 5.1** Considerations for Pairing Teachers One On One

| Considerations for pairing teachers one on one | | |
|---|---|---|
| Mentoring | Special educators' high levels of motivation typically make them a wonderful candidate for mentoring relationships. | → **Consider pairing special educators with first-year teachers or teachers who are new to the school.** They will effectively support them in navigating the school environment and will keep them positive and solution-oriented when challenges arise. |
| Coaching | Special educators' general goal-focused working style makes them prime candidates for instructional coaches. | → **Consider pairing special educators with teachers who have become stagnant in their professional growth or teachers who perform at a high level but are apathetic about trying new things.** Their focus on goals and achievement of them will allow them to uncover alternate ways to achieve the end results and thereby provide a fresh perspective for their colleague. |
| Co-teaching | Special educators' knowledge and resourcefulness can be incredibly effective when thinking about the vertical alignment of skills across grade levels as well as knowledge on instructional techniques that will increase student engagement and comprehension of the material. | → **Consider pairing special educators with general educators who have solid instruction and regularly show student growth with the average student in their class.** The special educator will be able to infuse new instructional strategies and support the expansion of knowledge for the co-teacher around students who are below or above grade level. |

In many buildings, the number of special educators is significantly less than the number of general educators and often these teachers' instructional load is spread across a series of grade levels. While it may seem like a good idea to spread the special educator in one way or another across all of the grade-level teams (e.g., rotate each week to a different grade-level meeting or spend 15 min with each grade level), this can result in a fractured experience

**Table 5.2** Considerations for Developing Team Structures

| Considerations for developing team structures | | |
|---|---|---|
| Small group (grade-level teams, PLCs) | Special educators' strength in collaboration and understanding of the vertical alignment of skills across grade levels make them great candidates to lead small group professional learning. | → **Consider the placement of special educators across grade-level teams.** While assigning special educators to work with multiple grade levels during small group meeting time may seem like a good way to spread their expertise, they may not be fully included on any team and their impact will only be surface level. Instead, placing special educators as coordinators of small group time will leverage their collaborative skills and allow them to introduce other teachers to the various tools that they use for instructional planning and delivery. |
| Schoolwide groups (ILTs, MTSS, and SIPs) | Special education teachers tend to possess strong skills in data analysis due to the constant use of data in their roles. | → **Consider including a special educator on all schoolwide teams.** Their strengths in data analysis can effectively support the data-driven planning in which schoolwide planning team regularly engage. |

for the special educator as well as for the teams with which they collaborate. Instead, reconsider the structure of your planning groups in order to maximize the special educators' involvement in a leadership capacity (Billingsley & Banks, 2019). Their collaborative and long-term planning skills are well suited for leading the professional learning in these small groups. Table 5.2 provides examples for small group leadership roles.

### Schoolwide Professional Development

Identifying the focus of professional development within a school often falls to the school leader who understands the macro-level view of all operations. Leading the professional growth of all educators within the building is a huge task, however, and one that often requires the support of additional leaders.

Special educators must regularly analyze standards across grade levels in order to better understand the complexity of instruction at each grade level, the scaffolding that could be applied, and the key skills and understandings that students must master to meet certain standards. This vertical depth of knowledge and analysis process could be leveraged at the schoolwide level to increase the overall coherence of instruction across grade levels. In order for teachers to plan for and deliver instruction with the appropriate amount of rigor, they must understand what skills students are arriving with and what they must have when they leave in order to be successful at the next grade level. Administrators could recruit special educators to support this vertical planning schoolwide to increase continuity for all instruction.

In addition, special educators' experience in goal planning gives them a unique ability to break down major school improvement plans into actionable steps. These steps translate into a cohesive professional development series. Special educators proactively identify misconceptions that the staff may have around the content of the sessions and integrate plans to address them. As instructional experts, special educators utilize professional development sessions to model new and effective instructional strategies with other adult learners. See Table 5.3 for additional details for utilizing special educators to support schoolwide professional development.

**Table 5.3** Considerations for Schoolwide Professional Development

| Considerations for schoolwide professional development | | |
|---|---|---|
| School-wide vertical alignment mapping | Special educators' content knowledge of how standards build on each other across grade levels could be used to increase continuity across grade levels. | → **Consider leveraging special educator's strengths in content knowledge to drive the initiation of schoolwide standards alignment.** Their knowledge and resourcefulness can be used to support the alignment of instruction across grade levels to increase continuity for students, to encourage cross grade-level collaboration, and to ensure appropriately rigorous instruction at all grade levels. |

*(Continued)*

**Table 5.3** Considerations for Schoolwide Professional Development (*Continued*)

| Considerations for schoolwide professional development | | |
|---|---|---|
| Long-term professional development plans | Special educators' strategic and purposeful nature could be used to plan, develop, and implement a long term aligned PD agenda. | → **Consider leveraging special educator's strengths in setting goals and developing achievable benchmarks to guide schoolwide professional development sessions that will build on each other over time.** Their individual student lens can easily be shifted to look at the needs of each individual teacher within a school community and in turn take the opinions of various stakeholders into account. |

## Summary

If we were to take an aerial view of a classroom, perhaps the first thing that would stand out is the clearly delineated, year-long instructional plan, developed and largely enacted by the general educator. Upon closer review, we will see the additional smaller, meandering, and dynamic paths surrounding the plan that show the wide variety of instructional routes that maybe in place for students in the classroom. These alternate paths have been designed by the special educator and represent the considerations that must be made for the different learning styles and needs of the students in the classroom.

The alternate paths showcase the instructional expertise of the special educator in their knowledge of individual students, content alignment across grade levels, and pedagogical strategies, all applied through an individual student lens. In order to design these paths, the special educator had to leverage their expert learning skills to effectively set and progress toward goals, use knowledge from their experience but also work to integrate new learning, and to stay motivated by the learning process.

Leaders can leverage their special educators' unique skill sets by placing them in various leadership positions. In such positions, they will balance individual teachers' areas of need through mentorship, coaching, or co-teacher pairings. They can model their skills in small group instructional leadership positions such as grade-level team leaders, instructional leadership team leaders, or school improvement team leaders. Finally, they may use their skills to serve all members of the school community by emphasizing and driving schoolwide professional development.

## Next Steps

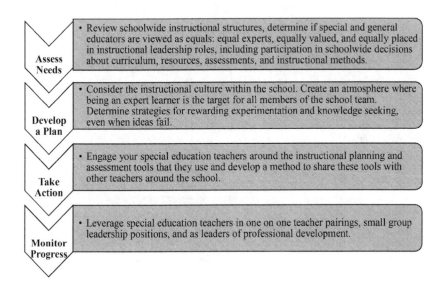

**Assess Needs**
• Review schoolwide instructional structures, determine if special and general educators are viewed as equals: equal experts, equally valued, and equally placed in instructional leadership roles, including participation in schoolwide decisions about curriculum, resources, assessments, and instructional methods.

**Develop a Plan**
• Consider the instructional culture within the school. Create an atmosphere where being an expert learner is the target for all members of the school team. Determine strategies for rewarding experimentation and knowledge seeking, even when ideas fail.

**Take Action**
• Engage your special education teachers around the instructional planning and assessment tools that they use and develop a method to share these tools with other teachers around the school.

**Monitor Progress**
• Leverage special education teachers in one on one teacher pairings, small group leadership positions, and as leaders of professional development.

## References

Alexander, P. A. (1992). Domain knowledge: Evolving themes and emerging concerns. *Educational Psychologist*, *27*(1), 33–51. https://doi.org/10.1207/s15326985ep2701_4

Benedict, A. E., Brownell, M. T., Park, Y., Bettini, E. A., & Lauterbach, A. A. (2014). Taking charge of your professional learning: Tips for cultivating special educator expertise. *TEACHING Exceptional Children*, *46*(6), 147–157. https://doi.org/10.1177/0040059914534618

Bettini, E., Benedict, A., Thomas, R., Kimerling, J., Choi, N., & McLeskey, J. (2017). Cultivating a community of effective special education teachers: Local special education administrators' roles. *Remedial and Special Education*, *38*(2), 111–126. https://doi.org/10.1177/0741932516664790

Billingsley, B., & Banks, A. (2019). Leadership for inclusive schools 1995–2015. In J. B. Crockett, B. Billingsley, & M. L. Boscardin (Eds.), *Handbook of leadership and administration for special education* (2nd ed., pp. 196–220). Routledge. https://doi.org/10.4324/9781315226378-13

CAST. (2018). *Universal design for learning guidelines version 2.2 [graphic organizer]*. Author. Retrieved fromhttp://udlguidelines.cast.org/binaries/content/assets/udlguidelines/udlg-v2-2/udlg_graphicorganizer_v2-2_numbers-yes.pdf

Chi, M. (2006). Two approaches to the study of experts' characteristics. In K. A. Ericcson, N. Charness, P. Feltovich, & R. Hoffman (Eds.), *The Cambridge handbook of expertise and expert performance* (1st ed., pp. 21–30). Cambridge, Cambridge University Press. https://doi.org/10.1017/cbo9780511816796.022

Cook, B. G., Haggerty, N. K., & Smith, G. J. (2019). Leadership and instruction: Evidence-based practices in special education. In J. B. Crockett, B. Billingsley, & M. L. Boscardin (Eds.), *Handbook of leadership and administration for special education* (2nd ed., pp. 353–370). Routledge. https://doi.org/10.4324/9781315226378-21

Hoppey, D., & McLeskey, J. (2013). A case study of principal leadership in an effective inclusive school. *The Journal of Special Education, 46*(4), 245–256. https://doi.org/10.1177/0022466910390507

Kotzee, B. (2014). Differentiating forms of professional expertise. In M. Young & J. Muller (Eds.), *Knowledge, expertise and the professions* (1st ed., pp. 61–77). Routledge.

Lindstrom, J. H. (2017). High-stakes testing and accommodations. In J. M. Kauffman, D. P. Hallahan, & P. C. Pullun (Eds.), *Handbook of special education* (2nd ed., pp. 447–460). Routledge. https://doi.org/10.4324/9781315517698-35

Meyer, A., Rose, D. H., & Gordon, D. (2014). *Universal design for learning: Theory and Practice.* CAST Professional Publishing.

Shulman, L. (1986). Those who understand: Knowledge growth in teaching. *Educational Researcher, 15*(2), 4–14. https://doi.org/10.3102/0013189X015002004

Sindelar, P. T., Wasburn-Moses, L., Thomas, R. A., & Leko, C. D. (2014). The policy and economic context of teacher education. In P. T. Sindelar, E. D. McCray, M. T. Brownell, & B. Lingnugaris/Kraft (Eds.), *Handbook of research on special education teacher preparation* (1st ed., pp. 3–16). Routledge. https://doi.org/10.4324/9780203817032.ch1

Stough, L. M., & Palmer, D. J. (2003). Special thinking in special settings: A qualitative study of expert special educators. *The Journal of Special Education, 36*(4), 206–222. https://doi.org/10.1177/002246690303600402

Zigmond, N. P. & Kloo, A. (2017). General and special education are (and should be) different. In J. M. Kauffman, D. P. Hallahan, & P. C. Pullun (Eds.), *Handbook of special education* (2nd ed., pp. 249–261). Routledge. https://doi.org/10.4324/9781315517698-21

# 6

# ADAPTIVE EXPERTISE

## Bryan Moles and Courtney Lynn Barcus

Administrators are called on to address a diverse set of school needs to meet both educational and organizational goals. The two thought processes below outline a need that administers often express and the expertise in problem solving exhibited by the special educator that could be applied at the schoolwide level.

| Administrator's Perspective | Special Educator's Perspective |
|---|---|
| The school board needs that report next week. I will need to meet with the clerk and the assistant principal about the budget, and the professional learning committee about School Improvement Plan. The way we are going about the plan just isn't working. We've been going in circles and hitting the same barriers; how can we turn this around? | I need to remember to meet with the IEP team next Monday. The data I'm collecting with this intervention strategy just isn't what I think we should be getting. The student also has another condition I am not familiar with, but I think we can work on these behaviors if we break them down. There's something we're not seeing here, we just need to change our angle. |

**Key Points:**

- **Understand** that **adaptive expertise** is developed using error and exception training as well as active learning through self-directed experimentation to create new knowledge that adeptly addresses novel situations.

- Realize that the procedures for **developing and implementing Individualized Education Plans**(IEPs) by a special educator are a scaled version of those same elements of training for adaptive expertise.
- **Leverage special educators and their unique skills** by applying them to schoolwide initiatives, in turn capitalizing on their adaptive expertise training to benefit the whole school population.

Adaptive expertise is a problem-solving approach with an emphasis on the creation of new knowledge and procedures to efficiently address novel situations. This new knowledge is produced through the thoughtful application of direct knowledge adaptive experts already have, routine knowledge, in novel ways and through observations of how events unfold. Adaptive experts forgo rigid decision paths, instead remaining responsive to data and the realities around them. By observing variations, tracking data, and using multiple perspectives, they engage in active learning during the process of their work, without direct oversight. As reflective decision makers, they can determine when the standard systems will suffice and when new procedures are required. Adaptive expertise is valued in both the private and public sectors because it enables individuals and teams to continue to perform at expert levels, even when faced with novel tasks.

Administrators, teachers, and all school staff are being called to answer challenges and problems beyond the scope of their traditional domains. At the same time, staff are being asked to stretch resources further and reach ever higher academic and functional goals – all while justifying choices with ample data along the way. To thrive in such a dynamic environment, school personnel must employ the strategies of adaptive expertise to evaluate their routines, forgoing outdated systems to create new knowledge and drive improvement. Adaptive expertise drives the individual to improvement through experimentation of relevant knowledge and the judicious allocation of resources. These experts can support school leaders and teams to effect important change and manage these new realities and pressures schools face. Luckily, there are highly trained teachers that have the disposition, perspective, and metacognitive skills who are readily available to guide this essential work: special educators.

When the established protocol no longer meets the process, though, or when a new problem demands attention, the same routines might become the problem, or fail to help solve the dilemma. This is not to say that routines are the antithesis of problem solving and improvement; having a set routine for a task and sticking to it builds adeptness in that routine. The process becomes facilitated by familiarity, taking up less mental energy. This 'routine expertise' is important in certain contexts, e.g., it is not possible to tackle every instance of classroom management like a new situation. The familiarity garnered through repetition and memory reduce the cognitive load to execute that task, freeing up attention to detail as well as improved performance at the task. If the standard procedure is meeting needs – and meeting those needs effectively – it does not need to be replaced. But, just as with any tool, routines often cannot meet every need. Adaptive expertise relies on using strategies to evaluate the existing decision rules and protocols in light of the available information on the task at hand. Beyond that, situations arise where no rules have been established for what to do. A new policy on teacher scheduling, novel initiatives for interventions, and other similar irregularities are examples of some of the situations school administrators find themselves facing with little routine knowledge for them to rely on. Utilizing adaptive expertise enables an individual to expand from their primary, initial domain to perform at high levels even when novel tasks and challenges present themselves. Special educators, through their experience in the special education process and supporting students with diverse needs, have learned to utilize these adaptive skills in their problem solving. School leaders can use this expertise to support schoolwide growth and adept problem-solving.

## The IEP Process: A Primer in Error Training

When a gap in knowledge is identified, the adaptive expert stands out in that they will review past choices and their resulting outcomes. In medicine, hospital groups and medical practices will conduct a postmortem, not just for when there is a death, but when a step-by-step analysis of the events related to one patient is useful to the larger group. These professionals analyze their systems to understand their programmatic processes. The medical field uses this as a time to reflect and evaluate what went well and what needs to be improved – how choices impacted outcomes and options later in the patient's care. Staff members do not lecture each other about strengths nor denigrate each other for poor outcomes, but every step of the process is seen as a chance to learn and hopefully improve for the next case. All choices become data points worthy of independent analysis that can be viewed outside reductive labels like good or bad, instead they are just data to be analyzed without judgment. Working together, staff members help each other engage in error analysis: Taking time to look where decisions led them, the variability of outcomes, and the options that remained to them along the way. These staff hope to use this analysis to better inform future decisions by learning from the past.

Similarly, in the business world, error management practices are a chance for a department or division to sit together and unpack the surrounding details around an event. All the choices made provide information on outcomes. The discussion does not dwell on labels of good or bad, but it takes each venture as a chance to learn. Labeling choices after the fact does not help the team, the decisions were made already. With an adaptive mindset, the team must be oriented toward improving performance, not rehashing mistakes. This process of dedicating time to analyzing previous choices in order to understand the impact of the choices made and improve the future choices is a central tenant of adaptive expertise.

Retrospective analysis is what enables adaptive experts to balance innovation against knowing when the tried and true method works. Evaluating what procedures work and which are not yielding as intended conserves resources. Adaptive experts are only able to do this because they are reverent to those tried methods and what those choices led to – without knowing what came before, adaptive experts cannot evaluate the routine (Cutrer et al., 2017).

The Individualized Education Plan (IEP) process operates in a similar vein: plans for each student are reevaluated at least annually. The goals and strategies implemented over the course of the previous year are appraised in light of the data collected. Here, the emphasis is not just on elucidating successful strategies; the focus is broadened to include looking at the entirety of the data and what lessons can be learned. All the data is considered, even for interventions that did not go as hoped – it is still a chance to observe the variability and see how the system worked. This is the data-based instruction discussed in Chapter 5 on instructional expertise that is not unique to special educators. What sets their adaptive expertise apart is their ability to parse out the elements and patterns in the facts, like helping staff conduct Functional Behavior Assessments (FBAs). These assessments must be living documents and only in the fullness of their observations can patterns emerge. The adaptive expert knows to break down the antecedent events and look at the functional outcomes of the following behaviors.

This reflective analysis in special education helps diverse teams of teachers and service providers see where they have been and what they have done, and, in turn, guides them toward where they need to go. Looking back, these teams compare direct intervention strategies, physical structures of supports, and staffing levels to ensure continued student access to the general education curriculum. Together, the team contemplates the entirety of the IEP as a system and works collaboratively to plan a way forward. This team is responding to what previous interventions were attempted – every year they build on what was done before, improving upon the progress already established or trying another direction.

**STOP AND REFLECT**

1. Before starting new initiatives, how does your school review what other schoolwide programs have been implemented?
2. How could your special education teachers support the utilization of this experience and knowledge?

These changes are the variables that adaptive experts study to gain systemic knowledge of a process. A special educator is not focused on a singular impact of a student's disability, but the system-wide implications that it might have. The student that is still struggling in a team-taught class, unless he or she receives significant one-on-one support from staff, might be a candidate for dedicated special education classes. A student's increased ability to utilize their assistive technology tools without staff support might lead to pulling back the use of assigned paraprofessionals in those classes where the data shows the student is succeeding without direct special education staff support. The team takes what was tried before, in light of data, to look ahead.

## Oriented Toward the Whole School

School Improvement Plans are one powerful example of how to capitalize on the adaptive expertise skills of a special educator to benefit schoolwide initiatives. Even for schools in large districts with central office support, there is local analysis of progress toward major goals that needs to be completed and reported out. Special educators are trained to manage data toward the evaluation of goals for students. The same procedures and goal-settings strategies they implement to support students receiving special education services are what schools are asked to do with their own growth: Setting measurable goals and plotting progress along the way. While the special educator might not be able to set the vision for the school or have all the answers for the School Improvement Plan, they will be able to contribute a clear process for reviewing and evaluating the goals. Together with their general education peers, they can help shape where the school can look to grow and identify leverage points for school initiatives. Special educators bring these skills in retrospective analysis, allowing them to be the method specialists necessary to help schools succeed.

## Collaborative Error Training

While seeking patterns in student work might be the norm for a special educator, changing the context from this individual student focus to the school environment might not be an easy transition. The educator might need support cultivating the confidence to excel at implementing the adaptive expertise they are trained in outside the classroom. A transitional space that can support the professional capital of the special educator and foster this skill in error training for all educators in a building is through Collaborative Assessment Clinics (CACs). The educators in these CACs review student work through a formal process to provide more in-depth error analysis. These clinics expound on the general conceptual practices of how special educators work to develop IEPs. The essential tasks of the CAC are largely familiar to the special educator and should tend to feel routine, but the peer educators included push the special educator to recast the practice as a communal endeavor. Resources on CACs can be found in Appendix B.

## Exception Training for Exceptional Learners

As researchers have conceptualized, a key value of adaptive expertise is the ability to maintain the delicate balance between exhaustive, constant innovation, and hazardous dedication to routine. The crux of this expertise is being aware of the nature of available resources, especially time and effort, and applying them to best address student needs. There are only so many hours in a day, and only so much time in a period for teachers to teach, so those minutes are precious. The speed and easiness afforded by routines has value because it conserves that precious time. Knowing when to use limited resources on novel methods – knowing that this problem can only be addressed with an exception to the rule – is a skill honed by adaptive experts as they reflect on previous problems and contemplate the outcomes.

Realizing that established routines are no longer meeting needs, the adaptive expert seeks out new systems and processes. Where error analysis is the deep-dive into choices made before, exception training uses that reflective knowledge to form decisions in the present and future. The adaptive expert turns their learning from previous problems to apply what they learned when faced with new problems. Informed by previous errors, the adaptive expert has a heightened awareness toward variables and unintended consequences from interventions.

Learning when to leave the established routine is not just direct instruction in every instance when the rule should not be applied. Reliance on memorizing every negative routine has the same pitfalls as any dedication to a routine. While some speed and automaticity is fostered by developing clear guidelines, these negative routines still inevitably fail to solve new problems. Researchers further caution that an emphasis on negative-case instruction is doubly dangerous, actually causing practitioners to be less aware of what was happening as they implement routines (Carbonell et al., 2014). Unable to adapt their mental models beyond the exact cases learned, researchers have found these negative routine procedures leave the individual with a reduced attention to details around the problem, inhibiting growth and learning. In overemphasizing all the instances of when not to follow the rule, the non-rule can become more limiting than the original. In a school setting, this aspect of adaptive expertise means special educators know that a student's diagnosis does not equate to a litany of negative decisions, a series of 'don't do this' and 'don't do that.' Students are unique and even with the same diagnosis, students can present with very different needs.

---

**STOP AND REFLECT**

1. How does your school realize when programmatic needs are not being met?
2. What systems would need to be put in place to ensure that schoolwide teams include a diverse make up (e.g., general educators, special educators, schoolwide staff, etc.)?
3. How can special educators help schoolwide teams address programmatic needs?

---

Adaptive experts do not employ this parochial categorization of when not to do something but remain responsive to data and past precedent to help guide them in recognizing exceptions as they depart from established routines. These experts make decisions not just based on an algorithmic reduction of the factors, but with reflective practice and attention to detail.

Special educators are these selfsame authorities on when new paths must be made; adaptive experts respond and develop a plan when the routine educational environment is not the appropriate environment for a student. Special educators pull the data and work with the entire educational team to recognize the hallmarks that indicate a nonroutine educational need. The general education teacher is not without his or her own resources, but the special educator is conscious of when a student's needs exceed what that one teacher and setting can offer. Special educators implement these strategies in small-scale environments during team teaching and also in highly individualized, innovative interventions. Students requiring a more structured check-in/check-out schedule for behavior can get the support they need on an individualized basis. And even on a smaller scale, in a team-taught physics class, special educators work with the content teacher to build supportive guided notes to keep everyone on task, utilizing universal design for learning (UDL) to support all student inclusion. Each of these students needed something beyond the typical standard classroom routine in order to help them show their learning and succeed.

### Oriented Toward the Whole School

When considering the whole school environment, exception training can be used to help guide decisions that balance innovation against established routine. Not every initiative in a school can or needs to be a breakthrough strategy produced by comprehensive analysis of every detail. Routines and established protocols have a place in facilitating efficiency. Special educators, reframing their classroom-wide emphasis, are able to evaluate and determine when routines meet the needs for the school. These same special educators will also support the team in realizing when the routines are no longer meeting the needs of the school.

The evaluative expertise that special educators can provide, helping balance between routine and innovation, is not a decision quickly made. Guided by data (see Chapter 3 for more information), the special educator evaluates the need for accommodations and modifications for students in their education plans and ensures the greatest access to the least restricted environment. Special education has the mandate that no student should be removed from the general education classroom more than is absolutely necessary, so special educators face balancing systems and placements as central to their work on IEP teams.

The adaptive expertise of a special educator can help the school leadership team and the broader school balance needs against resources to maximize outcomes for the given initiative. This could help in building schedules that assure student and staff needs are met, or reviewing curricular resources for alignment with school mission and academic standards. The special educator may also support the team in realizing when the school needs more support and in turn may support the development of grant applications or may help establish community partnerships. As trained consumers of data, special educators are taught when additional steps and resources are necessary for success.

### Promoting Exception Training

Just as CACs support teachers in better analyzing error training, when teachers continue those collaborative conversations to include discussions of next steps, the larger group has a chance to learn from the outcomes of those decisions. For example, discussing adaptations to address antecedent events for unwanted conditions and continuing to update the group on implementation and success allows everyone to learn from that unique case. Following the problem-solving process provides more examples for teachers to learn from and exceptions to reflect on in their own practice and classrooms. By vocalizing their thought process and walking themselves and others through the steps they take, special educators can cultivate greater comfort with the process, and greater comfort with exposing themselves in the process. This comfort supports the special educator in developing their professional voice among peers. With this confident voice, special educators are better able to advocate for exceptions to the traditional school routines in schoolwide contexts and support leadership teams to ensure improved growth.

## Active Learning through Self-Directed Work

Adaptive experts, in order to be truly useful in error training and exception analysis, must also be reflective of their own knowledge and where it falls short. What use is a retrospective investigation without deep knowledge around the matter at hand? How does acknowledging an exceptional situation help unless it is followed up with a knowledge-driven intervention? Adaptive experts are motivated to expand their own understanding, not as directed but as independently motivated learners (Ford & Schmidt, 2000).

Every year, special educators face a new caseload of students, each a unique learner with an IEP. As was outlined in Chapter 5, there is no textbook for special education, no easy handouts, and no curriculum for the year with lesson plans that divvy up what the special educator is to cover. It is the responsibility of the special educator to seek out what knowledge they need to ensure student success. They have to reflect on their caseload, looking at the unique needs of their students and assess their own knowledge gaps to evaluate where they need to seek more knowledge.

Year after year, the field of special education is also changing. New interventions, new pedagogies, and new tools are developed, but they are not the subject of textbooks like a general education classroom. Mathematics research leads to new math curricula and textbook series for entire grade bands, in special education the breadth of student needs precludes this *en masse* effect. Instead the special educator must always respond to the novel needs of the student population currently before them.

As discussed in Chapter 1, the reality of special educator preparation programs is that they cannot prepare their candidates with the discrete knowledge for every special education context or need. There is no clearly delineated content like linear algebra or cultures of Mesopotamia. The field of special education is too broad, too all-encompassing for any preparation program to distill into a handful of college years. Instead, programs instill in their special educators the tools and wherewithal to expand their own content knowledge in response to student needs for the educator's entire career – they must be independently motivated learners.

Special educators also know to rely on team knowledge, garnered through collaboration, to expand their own mastery of content and systems. Each member of the team provides their own specific knowledge and the special educator, using their adaptive expertise, works with the team to piece it all together. Special educators realize they cannot know it all, that no one staff member or team member can have all the answers, but together the team's collective know how exceeds the individual.

## Oriented Toward the Whole School

The adaptive expert is prized in business and medicine because they realize when their current knowledge does not meet the current need. Without prompting, they self-assess and respond to knowledge-based needs without being instructed or guided by others. This self-directed exploration sets the adaptive expert apart and is largely what enables them to excel even in the face of novel tasks. Special educators have this same self-driven ability to learn. The special educator is taught from their earliest teacher preparation classes that they cannot learn everything, that the very nature of their profession and the students they serve demand lifelong learning to meet their needs.

For school administrators, this self-direction is essential in light of the ever-increasing demands on schools and leadership. Federal, state, and district initiatives clamor for ever-greater proportions of administrator time, and still there are the school needs that require attention. Special educators, with their ability to work toward their own learning needs, can prove invaluable on school teams for their ability to support systemic team learning without the need for direct supervision or guidance.

Special educators, because of their training and experience as adaptive experts, have the self-regulation to reflect on their own knowledge and skills, as well as the knowledge and skills of their teams. Like working with the IEP team, special educators have to work collaboratively to promote learning from a range of specialists to meet student needs. When the knowledge needs of the team cannot be met internally, the special educator knows they have to seek the information themselves. This is the important step that delineates the problem-solving prowess of the adaptive expert, the self-regulation goes beyond just reflection: the special educator seeks learning and new tools without direct instruction or prompting. While general educators can face similar situations at times with their classes, the scale of self-directed knowledge seeking special educators must engage in covers the breadth of disabilities covered by IDEA (De Arment et al., 2013).

Tasked with responding to new state curricular needs on the school instructional leadership team, the special educator can provide the reflection necessary to see where the team's understanding of the new curricula needs support. Without direct instructions to do so, the special educator searches for resources the team can use to improve their knowledge. The special educator does not hoard their knowledge, but ensures the whole school benefits from their learning. Trained through the special education process and versed in collaborative team-based knowledge building, special educators prove a unique asset to their school leadership teams.

### Fostering Independent Learning

Professional Learning Communities (PLCs) provide a great opportunity to help develop an educator's skills in active learning through unguided research while retaining that classroom emphasis that is familiar. The PLC is a teacher-based group in a school or group of schools that gather together for individual and group-oriented professional learning. The staff members choose a general topic they want to explore that provides a general theme or arc to the learning series. What each teacher researches is self-determined and this agency fosters independent learning. Individual members contribute articles and other informational sources that they have researched that illustrate a facet of that general theme. Working collaboratively, the team sets timelines and establishes norms for how information is shared in a way that can be meaningful and impactful on individual professional practice.

An important aspect of PLCs that supports the independent learning of educators is the reflective nature fostered by the group dynamic. This interpersonal dialogue aligns with the internal processes that special educators engage in when exercising adaptive expertise. In talking about learning, discussing prior learning and assessing current knowledge to address needs, educators can work collaboratively to implement new knowledge and benefit students. PLCs can help keep teams accountable and focused. Check Appendix B for more resources on PLCs and other collaborative teacher groups that could benefit your school.

### Reframing the Premise

Sometimes the past does not prove a useful guide. Sometimes understanding that something new must be implemented is not enough. Sometimes knowing what you need to learn does not make the answers more clear. There are times when a team can become bogged down with how to conceptualize not only a problem, but their perceptions of each element of the problem. These restrictions inhibit the team's ability to access all their group knowledge that could be useful for finding a solution. It is at these times that reframing the premise, taking a different vantage point or even accepting multiple perspectives, is what enables the adaptive expert to excel at finding solutions.

Individuals and teams can get stuck in a rut. Not just in how they complete a task, growing comfortable in a routine, but also in how they conceptualize and visualize tasks. Researchers have found that the process we use to mentally represent a task or problem begins to lock down what knowledge is accessed to address the task (Joung et al., 2006). In certain contexts, individuals and teams expect to access certain domains of knowledge to solve problems. Every mental coding of the situation connects to a certain framework and set of facts. Those connections can become siloed and forced into repeated measures. The application of those definitions to the elements of a task can create narrow routines for how the task is approached, both building speed and familiarity, but also leading a team down a routine path of what knowledge is brought to bear on the problem. If the initial perspective on the problem helps the team to work out a solution, we would consider that a win, but what happens when the solution does not succeed? When researching how medical students addressed problems and the learning these students accessed, researchers found that the students were often unaware of how the routines had conditioned them and the narrow slice of their learning they were utilizing to solve the problems.

Consider Edward Boring's (1930) drawing that is at once a portrait of his wife and mother-in-law. The dual image depicts two different scenes and characters depending on what features are in focus to our eyes. When you first saw it, did you see a young woman with a feather in her hair or an old woman with a headscarf? If you saw the young woman, did your eyes focus on certain features, and did your mind begin to access thoughts, memories, and connected information to that image? When seeing the old woman, did your mind follow a different path, accessing different memories and thoughts? The same lines draw both images, but the focus completely alters the meaning of the lines and what is in our minds when we behold the image. In instant associations such as this, our minds make narrow the information we actively access and foreground certain thoughts and memories above others.

---

### STOP AND REFLECT

1. Are there initiatives or tasks in your school that have stalled out?
2. How has the team addressed this stalled progress?
3. How do special educators work with school teams to provide essential perspective, or helping seek new perspectives, to support initiatives and improved progress?

---

Just as the adaptive expert has the tools to realize when a routine is no longer meeting their needs, these experts also know when the perception of a situation is narrowing what knowledge and tools they are accessing. In reframing the premise, the adaptive expert breaks down the barriers to accessing all the knowledge that can help them address the problem. When free to access the full breadth of their knowledge, adaptive experts reach better solutions. Similarly, special educators must often reframe the perspective they themselves as educators and administrators have around their students and their students' abilities, no more so than when conducting behavior analyses. Part of a special educator's job is to conduct behavior analyses in response to problematic student behaviors. At first blush, a student that continuously disrupts a mathematics class could just be demonstrating his or her dislike of the subject. Suspending this first perspective, though, the special educator reframes their interpretation of the behaviors. Viewing the student's actions under the premise of a masking behavior – the student acting up to hide his or her own difficulties with the content – the special educator begins correlating the instances with specific content days. Having reframed the nature of the behaviors, the special educator can appropriately address the antecedent conditions for the student and provide the supports the student requires to meet their needs and succeed in the classroom.

When special educators work with their general education collaborators on adapting lessons or planning co-taught instruction, they are implementing this same reframing to support student needs. The special educators are using their adaptive expertise to facilitate a wider perception of the lesson, the types of sensory input, the forms of sensory responses and the perception both teachers have around the ideal implementation of the lesson. By recasting how teachers perceive the elements of the lesson, they are better able to distill the essential elements and ensure access to these points for all learners.

### *Oriented Toward the Whole School*

School administrators have access to amounts of data that could not be imagined a generation ago. At the same time, administrators are expected to derive new meanings and new initiatives from the data with few data scientists at their call. Here the special educator can help reframe the data, and keep the team's knowledge fluid around it.

The special educator's skill in retaining flexible connections to their own knowledge and the team's knowledge ensures that singular data points are not monolithic facts but composites of individuals that every team member can help define. The special educator can reframe the data to help the team start to see patterns and begin forming next steps.

The special educator's ability to utilize multiple perspectives is also useful to reframe approaches to difficult situations or initiatives. Special educators cannot see their students as a litany of what the student cannot do, concentrating on the negative. The mindset of cannot: 'cannot do this,' 'cannot do that,' 'don't perform well with this,' and 'can't even begin to understand that,' ensures that there is little the students will do. The special educator must reframe their reference to focus on the positive, the student's strengths, thus identifying where the student can expand rather than what they 'cannot.'

This same ability can help school teams remain positive in their work and reject an emphasis of deficits while working together.

### Supporting the Reframing Process

Like this section outlines, when special educators analyze student actions to establish the components of the behaviors, from antecedent to consequence, that individual attention to key elements helps them reframe their perspective. Almost like another form of error analysis, when considering segments separately and then in context adaptive experts are able to ensure that perceptions based off context do not limit the knowledge accessed. Leaders can support the adaptive expertise of their teachers in this domain by providing venues to discuss and explore problem solving in teams. Branching out from the domain of the CAC but utilizing a similar procedure to enable analysis on multiple levels, providing space and time for teachers to talk and problem solve together supports their ability to gain multiple perspectives on problems. As the teachers build confidence in analyzing the features of problems, leadership can start leaning on this team to support their own problem solving for schoolwide initiatives.

## Professional Capital

An important consideration when asking any professional to reorient their practice to a new sphere with colleagues is the idea of professional capital. Professional capital is not a direct monetarization or compensation for work, the term refers to capital in that it carries with it the idea of something built up and then expended. Professional in that it is cultivated in the employment arena through comfort and confidence in one's own content and in the relationships with coworkers. Professional capital can be viewed as how someone's professional confidence influences their relationships with coworkers. When asking special educators to recast their adaptive expertise from a student-centered domain to the schoolwide and collaborate with peer educators in a new fashion, it is important to realize that this will require a certain amount of professional capital. Special educators might be versed in using these adaptive expertise principals in their own practices and classrooms, but when asked to utilize them for schoolwide problems with their general education peers it requires not only their comfort with the expertise, but the professional confidence to continue what they know.

## Summary

Special educators are not a cure for every problem that a school might have. Their first day leading a team will not lead to ground-breaking innovations that alter the field forever. But what special educators do bring to the table is adaptive expertise. Because of their training in special education procedures and practices, these educators have been instructed in the same processes and systems that researchers have seen improve how teams and individuals handle novel situations. The error analysis that helps medical teams improve their patient outcomes is how special educators work to ensure student progress on goals. Special educators work to recognize exceptions to keep their students from falling behind. They understand that they have to keep learning to meet the needs of ever more diverse students, and appearances can belie what is really going on. The very nature of special education is to adjust to changing circumstances and do it well.

Adaptive expertise is what helps effective special educators perform at high levels year after year, even though every year is a novel group of students and situations. Their training in preparatory programs as well as the realities of day-to-day special education means that these tenets of adaptive expertise are reinforced and utilized every day and can be used to support work outside their classrooms. Utilized in schoolwide initiatives and working in teams with other school staff, special educators are able to bring these adaptive expertise skills to bear to aid the problem solving of the whole school community.

## Next Steps

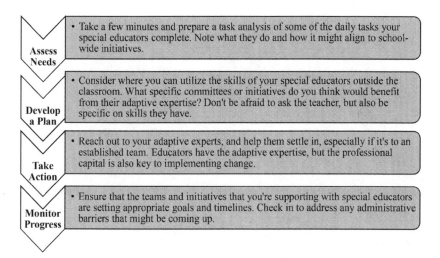

**Assess Needs**
- Take a few minutes and prepare a task analysis of some of the daily tasks your special educators complete. Note what they do and how it might align to schoolwide initiatives.

**Develop a Plan**
- Consider where you can utilize the skills of your special educators outside the classroom. What specific committees or initiatives do you think would benefit from their adaptive expertise? Don't be afraid to ask the teacher, but also be specific on skills they have.

**Take Action**
- Reach out to your adaptive experts, and help them settle in, especially if it's to an established team. Educators have the adaptive expertise, but the professional capital is also key to implementing change.

**Monitor Progress**
- Ensure that the teams and initiatives that you're supporting with special educators are setting appropriate goals and timelines. Check in to address any administrative barriers that might be coming up.

## References

Boring, E. G. (1930). A new ambiguous figure. *The American Journal of Psychology, 42*(3), 444–445. http://doi.org/10.2307/1415447

Carbonell, K. B., Stalmeijer, R. E., Könings, K. D., Segers, M., & van Merriënboer, J. J. (2014). How experts deal with novel situations: A review of adaptive expertise. *Educational Research Review, 12*, 14–29. https://doi.org/10.1016/j.edurev.2014.03.001

Cutrer, W. B., Miller, B., Pusic, M. V., Mejicano, G., Mangrulkar, R. S., Gruppen, L. D., Hawkins, R. E., Skochelak, S. E., & Moore Jr, D. E. (2017). Fostering the development of master adaptive learners: A conceptual model to guide skill acquisition in medical education. *Academic Medicine*, *92*(1), 70–75. https://doi.org/10.1097/acm.0000000000001323

De Arment, S. T., Reed, E., & Wetzel, A. P. (2013). Promoting adaptive expertise: A conceptual framework for special educator preparation. *Teacher Education and Special Education*, *36*(3), 217–230. https://doi.org/10.1177/0888406413489578

Ford, J. K., & Schmidt, A. M. (2000). Emergency response training: Strategies for enhancing real-world performance. *Journal of Hazardous Materials*, *75*(2–3), 195–215.

Joung, W., Hesketh, B., & Neal, A. (2006). Using "war stories" to train for adaptive performance: Is it better to learn from error or success? *Applied Psychology*, *55*(2), 282–302. http://dx.doi.org/10.1111/j.1464-0597.2006.00244.x

# 7

# COLLABORATION

## Kasandra Posey, Krista McGrath, and Geraldo Tobon

The school district selected your school as a pilot site to implement a new program focused on improving student literacy. The program uses a systematic approach to providing student supports that focuses on the delivery of the strongest practices at the classroom, small group, and individualized levels depending on student needs. In order to ensure all students receive appropriate support, the district mandated the development of a schoolwide literacy team to assist with the selection, implementation, and evaluation of effective literacy practices. When presenting the proposal, district personnel present research that shows the development of schoolwide teams is essential for improved problem-solving and developing teacher buy-in. For the literacy initiative, and team, to be successful, the school needs to enhance the culture of collaboration to support the adoption and implementation of effective literacy strategies.

| Administrator perspective | Staff perspective |
| --- | --- |
| We will finally be able to reach students at all levels. This process will allow my staff to work together to improve reading instruction for all students regardless of their level of need. We should see great improvements in student academic performance on next year's standardized tests. | I would love to join the schoolwide literacy team, but I just do not see where I can fit the time to meet with a team in my already full schedule. I wish there was a way to make more time so that I can contribute and ensure all students have access to the most effective reading supports available. |

**Key Points:**

- Create a **culture of collaboration** within your school to build a strong foundation of teaming practices.
- **Support collaboration** through a variety of practices such as modeling, team looping, and professional development.
- Improve **student outcomes** and **community relations** by utilizing **special educators as leaders** of collaboration.

Collaborative experiences are abundant in both our personal and professional lives. Consider the relationship you have with your doctor, mechanic, or babysitter. How about meeting a deadline for a work project with your coworkers, planning an event for creating new initiatives within your school organization, or making decisions on your school's goals? While you work to accomplish a goal with these individuals, collaboration must take place. Moreover, in today's schools, there has been a huge push for collaboration among students, faculty, community organizations, and other agencies. Essential to school improvement is our understanding of the important role collaboration plays in ensuring all students receive the supports needed to meet their academic and behavioral potential. As school personnel continue to seek improved reform practices, collaboration is at the center of nearly all of these efforts.

In order to ground the information in this chapter, it is important to provide a definition of collaboration that encompasses its multifaceted meaning and application. With that in mind, we are defining collaboration as: The collective interactions of individuals in a group on a shared task or activity to accomplish a common goal that otherwise cannot be accomplished by one individual. This definition of collaboration involves unity, ownership, and accountability. It is important to recognize that collaboration happens *with* someone *on* something; it is a way of doing something. Friend and Cook (2010) identify collaboration as a style. As you dig deeper into this chapter, consider the ways that schools work together to support all students and accomplish established goals. Provided in this chapter is a brief overview of the history of collaboration in schools, an example of how special educators collaborate continually with colleagues to meet the needs of students, and considerations for administrators to support increased collaboration and leadership for special educators.

## History of Collaboration in Schools

To get a better sense of the importance of collaboration, it is necessary to understand the role collaboration has played in schools in the past.

Autonomy was, and to an extent, continues to be valued by educators (Pearson & Moomaw, 2005). That is, school personnel take ownership of their students, their class environments, and student outcomes, among a host of other responsibilities. Historically, most teachers taught in isolation without the support or benefit of colleagues. Teaching was often viewed as an individual endeavor where teachers consider their students as their sole responsibility. School reform aimed at improving academic and social outcomes for all students has led to changes in the extent to which teachers and other school personnel collaborate in today's schools. More rigorous educational standards and the need to provide all students with a free and appropriate education, including students who have been disadvantaged in the educational system, require increased collaboration to ensure successful implementation of school initiatives. For instance, the emphasis on inclusive education in which students with disabilities receive more of their education in the general education classroom requires a team of individuals to create an Individualized Educational Plan (IEP) that meets the needs of each student with a disability. The need for IEP teams is not just best practice (Hoover & Teeters, 2019; Pellegrino et al., 2015) but it is mandated through the Individuals with Disabilities Act (IDEA). Other examples of collaboration in schools include the use of grade-level teams, teams for school improvement, response-to-intervention (RTI) or Multi-Tiered Systems of Support (MTSS) teams, social emotional learning, and Positive Behavior Intervention Support (PBIS) teams. Each of these teams requires school personnel to work together and collaborate to address a particular area of need to ensure student success. In the spirit of inclusive practice, collaboration has filtered into many more classrooms and influenced how educators innovate, provide instruction, and hone their skills.

Students in special education, and their teachers, often find themselves isolated from other members of the school community. However, the emphasis on serving students in the Least Restrictive Environment (LRE) requires strategic planning to improve the integration of students with disabilities into the common structures and culture of a school. For instance, special educators must collaborate with a range of stakeholders including general education teachers, speech pathologists, physical therapists, social workers, families, and other staff within a school building to ensure the student's IEP is implemented with fidelity. As such, special educators are often the primary collaborator within a school. As you look to weave collaboration into the fabric of your school, special educators have demonstrated expertise and can provide others with an opportunity to work together to meet the needs of the school's most vulnerable students.

**STOP AND REFLECT**

Consider the experiences that you have had with collaboration in your professional history:

1. What experiences have encouraged and supported collaboration between yourself and others? What were the key features that allowed for this collaboration to be successful?
2. What experiences have you had where collaboration felt difficult to achieve? What barriers did you or your team face?

## Collaboration Benefits All

The shift toward more collaborative schools will not only benefit students with disabilities, but it has the potential of benefiting all students (Ronfeldt et al., 2015). Today's schools are more diverse than ever. Students from a variety of cultural and linguistic backgrounds, country of origin, and ability make up the school population. The prevalence of students with disabilities in today's schools requires professionals with a variety of expertise to collaborate to ensure all students are provided with a quality education. When students require a comprehensive set of services or have a variety of needs, the educators serving these students must engage in some form of collaboration. For example, a special educator working in a mainstream classroom will best meet the needs of these students through consistent collaboration with the general education teacher and other related service providers such as the speech and language pathologist, social worker, and school psychologist. While there may be several individuals supporting the implementation of a student's IEP, a constant throughout special education is the need to collaborate across a wide swath of professionals and family members.

## How Administrators Create a Culture of Collaboration

The diverse needs of students in today's schools requires a school culture that is committed to and promotes collaboration. How schools engage in collaborative practices varies depending on the needs of the school. Administrators are tasked with establishing a culture of collaboration within their schools. To support effective collaboration across the school, policies and practices must highlight collaboration as imperative. While changing the culture of a school can be a lengthy and difficult process, collaboration provides the basis for ensuring that all individual students, no matter their ability level, are provided with a high-quality education.

How then should administrators begin to re-culture their school to support effective and meaningful collaboration? Meaningful collaboration can be accomplished through building capacity within the school building. Capacity encompasses all things that contribute to the fabric of a school including the school climate and visions, scheduling, staffing, as well as a school's finances (Waldron & McLeskey, 2010). At the core of developing capacity for collaboration within your school are six fundamental principles:

- Develop school teams to focus on core instructional, behavioral, and engagement initiatives.
- Provide space so every member's input and expertise are valued.
- Model a culture in which collaboration is valued.
- Develop structures where all members of the school community can participate.
- Make clear teams are accountable for outcomes.
- Support all team members' understanding of collaboration.

Keeping these principles in mind, can help administrators develop a culture of collaboration by emphasizing its importance in the school's mission and vision, providing structures that promote collaboration, and by highlighting and modeling collaboration to school personnel. Given their experience working with a range of stakeholders including general education teachers, parents and families, and related service providers, special educators can assist in this endeavor (see Chapter 2 for more details). Each of these principles is at the heart of the special educator's work. In order to illustrate the important role that special educators play in schoolwide collaboration, co-teaching and collaboration with families and community members are used as two examples where special educators demonstrate and develop their collaborative skill.

## Co-Teaching

Co-teaching refers to an instructional model in which a general educator and a special educator share instructional responsibilities to ensure students with disabilities receive appropriate educational supports within the LRE. Co-teaching provides an opportunity for students with disabilities to receive needed supports while also working alongside their peers without disabilities. While co-teaching is enticing because it increases access and equity for student with disabilities, successful implementation requires close collaboration between the general education and special educator to ensure lesson plans account for both the instructional content and adaptations to ensure student success (Cook et al., 2017). By adopting co-teaching as a school instructional model, administrators can establish a culture of collaboration. The natural collaboration that occurs through co-teaching partnerships has the potential to spark greater interest in collaboration within other spheres and across other stakeholders.

Dieker (n.d.) outline considerations for establishing a successful co-teaching instructional model. In particular, these authors emphasize the need for administrators to provide collaborating educators with (a) planning time, (b) consistent grading policies, (c) opportunities to ready students to learn within co-teaching structures, (d) time to learn about the co-teaching model and its implementation to their particular classroom, and (e) adequate time to plan for assessment including progress monitoring and considering issues related to high-stakes testing.

## Planning Time

Co-teaching teams need specific, dedicated time to do their work. Essential to their success is that their co-planning time is scheduled out *first*. Administrators and teachers should schedule other important duties around co-planning. This time is important in order to not just co-plan, but build rapport and ensure there is active communication.

## Grading Policies

The assessment of students with disabilities is often different than those applied to students without disabilities. It's imperative that teachers come to terms at the start of a year so as to be on the same page regarding the grading policies, academic expectations, and overall learning goals for all students. This will allow for consistency, which will best serve their co-teaching relationship.

## Student Readiness

As schools move toward a more inclusive setting for students, personnel, and administration must be aware that students with disabilities might not have experience in general education settings. Likewise, their peers might not have experience learning in an inclusive environment. As such, students with and without disabilities might benefit from additional support to prepare them to learn in an inclusive classroom. Strong co-teaching teams will implement a plan to address these needs.

## Teacher Readiness

The notion of co-teaching can cause resistance at times because, simply put, teachers may be used to working alone and taking accountability solely for their own curricular plans. Teachers should be allowed autonomy as they implement co-teaching while also being prepared to be collectively responsible. Some teachers will be more ready than others, and it is important to provide teachers with appropriate space to work this out.

## Assessment Practices

While high-stakes testing can provide a lens with which to evaluate the success of inclusive environments, we cannot rely on those to inform daily practice. Administrators and educators must be constantly evaluating the success of each classroom with co-teaching. Teachers should be gathering data as to the academic and behavioral growth of all students to ensure growth is sufficient across the board, and ensure there are enough supports in place for all students, with or without disabilities. School leaders should be a part of this evaluation of data, specifically looking at all vulnerable populations, not just those within a special education setting. Schools leaders should also consider informal data such as student interviews in inclusive settings to ascertain their sense of success.

## Collaborating with Family and Community Members

Collaboration among teachers through co-teaching is just one example of the cooperative role that special educators assume within a school. Collaboration, of course, extends beyond working with colleagues at school to ensure the implementation of effective practices. Special educators must also develop relationships with other key stakeholders including parents, guardians, and family members of students. Moreover, special educators often work to engage members of the community to develop opportunities and experiences for students with disabilities. From a special education perspective, these stakeholders need to share in the responsibility of educating students with disabilities. For good reason too, according to Buffenbarger et al. (2011, para 41), 'when schools, parents, families, and communities work together to support learning, students tend to earn higher grades, attend school more regularly, stay in school longer, and enroll in higher level programs.' This is true regardless of the education level of parents, family income or background, and a variety of community factors. While some states have gone as far as drafting policies requiring the collaboration of schools and families, it is at times overlooked in the discussion of the important, collaborative role that special educators play in ensuring appropriate and meaningful educational plans for students with disabilities.

Regarding parental involvement, special educators must work in concert with parents to ensure the school is meeting their child's needs and to develop and implement meaningful supports. Developing a positive rapport with parents is sometimes challenging and requires building trust through communication, sincerity, and understanding. Many parents experience barriers to engaging in the special education process and feeling empowered to be active participants in their child's education. Some parents may not feel equipped to get involved, may have busy schedules, or may simply feel uncomfortable based on their own school histories or perceived knowledge of instructional, behavioral, or functional expectations. There may be cultural or language barriers, and at times families may feel school staff do not understand their experiences. For some parents, involvement with their child's education might look different, where the involvement takes place primarily at home; however, special educators are trained to not dismiss these issues and to actively engage all parents regardless of their hesitations or concerns because of the importance of parental contributions to the special education process. To learn more about advocacy and the ways in which special educators collaborate with parents around issues of advocacy see Chapter 8 on 'Advocacy.'

Following the lead of the special educator, school administrators and teachers can learn concrete ways to engage family members and community stakeholders. For instance, administrators can start by providing professional development to teachers on a range of strategies to engage parents, families, and community members. Using the special educator as a collaboration expert, school personnel may learn about strategies to engage these external partners and glean important information from parents, families, and community members. The special educator can provide leadership around the development of actionable goals to bridge current gaps in collaboration policy and practice. For instance, information about parental perceptions on the extent to which the school is meeting the needs of students can be gathered through parent nights, workshops, surveys, and through various other activities such as assemblies, parent-teacher conferences, and community nights. Special educators can use their experiences and expertise to focus on improving communication with families and to develop partnerships with community liaisons. In the following section, a more detailed overview of the ways in which special educators can be used to lead the development of collaborative policies and practices on across school stakeholders is provided.

## Special Educators as Collaborative Experts

Through developing high-quality co-teaching partnerships and extending collaboration to families and members of the community, a culture of collaboration will start to emerge. A collaborative culture is essential because of its impacts on student academic and behavioral outcomes. Research suggests that increased collaboration impacts student outcomes, especially for students with disabilities (Cook & Friend, 1991; Friend & Cook, 1990; Haycock, 2007; Hernandez, 2013). Due to the nature of their work with and for students with disabilities, special educators are collaborative leaders. As collaborative leaders, they support teaming with a variety of school staff. Their work with families, school psychologists, speech pathologists, social workers, and other members of the school community is indicative of their abilities to lead other school-based groups. Consider how a special educator could use the knowledge gained from their everyday work of co-planning with other teachers, related service providers, and other key stakeholders such as families and community. These experiences highlight key collaborative skills necessary to lead or chair a schoolwide Professional Learning Community (PLC), MTSS committee, or an Instructional Leadership Team (ILT). Special educators consistently work with teams across the community, depending on student needs; this skill set is paramount when trying to develop strong schoolwide teams.

How schools engage with families and their community partners impacts student outcomes. While many may see these as separate entities these groups must remain intricately involved. What does this mean? This means that active engagement from all parties for educational enhancement is key to the advancement of school staff, students, families, and communities. Thinking outside the box and understanding who constitutes family opens up a wide array of family groups including, aunts, uncles, grandparents, etc. This same thinking speaks to how one look at a community, the local grocery stores, religious organizations, the park district, community centers, Young Men's Christian Association (YMCA), gyms, barber and beauty salons, etc. Making connections with these groups supports student development through earlier career planning, support with academic development through tutoring options that may be available within the community, wraparound services, etc. Community and family involvement provide a level of social service support critical to the academic achievement of all learners.

Van Roekel (2008) notes that when school districts are looking to improve student achievement, they often overlook the role that the community and family partnerships can play in school reform. Much of the earlier literature speaks to the importance of education as a function of society. Allowing special educators to lead the charge only acts as an extension of their work. As an administrator, ensuring that the many barriers identified by partners, to the best of your organization's ability are resolved will work in your school's favor. Learning does not just happen in schools; therefore, the support of families and the community is key.

Special educators could also lead the charge for improved school-community relations. They are responsible for implementing services for some students that require community-based instruction, this means that special educators are responsible for developing partnerships with agencies, organizations, and businesses within the community to aid in meeting student needs. With the knowledge gained as community collaborators, special educators could lead or chair a community engagement committee for the school as a whole. Making community connections not only benefits students with disabilities but also plays a role in connecting all students with the supports they require outside of the school. These connections could also build relationships with families, as the school will be able to offer supports beyond student learning.

## How Administrators Can Support Collaboration

Moving toward increased collaboration in a school can be accomplished with careful consideration, planning, and implementation. Utilizing the steps below can assist in developing a culture of collaboration in your school in which all students, but in particular, students with disabilities are supported. Administrators might find it helpful to tap into the key skills special educators have that are needed for effective collaboration. While some of the areas below require a shift in thinking, maintaining that your special educator leaders are available and equipped with the knowledge and expertise to help drive this initiative will prove advantageous for your school at large.

### Identify Key Leaders

Not all staff within a school must be leaders. Identifying characteristics that align with the schoolwide vision and articulating this to staff, helps administrators determine who is a key leader. Being vigilant of the work that special educators engage in on a daily basis may excite opportunities to build their leadership capacity in a way that will prove beneficial to the school as a whole with a focus on students with disabilities. When administrators can select staff that is in line with the collaborative schoolwide visions, they can further push the agenda of this type of a school environment. What starts as one individual's dream can become the collective vision with the right school leaders in place.

### Establish Professional Learning Communities

PLCs refer to a group of educational professionals that meet regularly to work collaboratively toward improving their practice and academic outcomes of students. While PLCs have become a popular buzzword understanding how to truly implement PLCs in schools as a critical practice is imperative. PLCs should help improve teaching practices. Special educators already have experience with collaboration as it is the epitome of their work. Effective PLC requires a clear purpose and direction. For instance, a PLC focused on improving teaching practices for students with disabilities needs to be focused on differentiation, using data to inform instruction, and evidenced-based practices to name a few topics. With the below strategies, special educators can help drive improved teaching and increased student academic achievement.

PLCs should involve conversations focused on how students learn and how teachers can best support. Ensuring that barriers that impact higher-level discussions between colleagues are also a key function for special educators who engage in collaborative practices on a regular basis. Special educators can leverage staff member's ability to identify and clearly define their roles in a PLC, ensuring that appropriate training is available to lead in PLCs and that all staff members understand each individual's intricate roles. Overall, ensuring that there is a consistent message about the purpose and roles of a PLC is messaged across the school can drive the change needed in instructional practices to promote consistent student growth. To learn more about special educators potential roles as PLC leaders, see Chapters 5 and 6.

### *Encourage Norm-Setting and Sharing of Goals*

Special educators consistently work with related service providers, families, and general education teachers to develop the most appropriate goals for students with IEPs. They also ensure that all staff are familiar with the student's goals. In addition, they are responsible for determining how to collect data on goals and who will be responsible for collecting this data. These are critical aspects of the IEP development and implementation process. Typically, special educators take the lead in IEP development and dissemination of its contents. Consider the special educator's expertise in these areas when thinking about schoolwide norm setting and goal sharing (see Chapter 2). As a schoolwide vision for a collaborative culture, special educators can use their skills garnered from their IEP team member experiences to support the realization of schoolwide goals. Their emphasis on advocating for children and families of children with disability makes them prime candidates to support in the development of norms and goals for the school (for more see Chapter 8). Including special educators on these planning teams will ensure that the school vision, norms, and goals are inclusive of students with disabilities and provide a high-quality special education program. Special educators continue to hone their skills in information sharing and goal setting and can use these skills for a more collective and comprehensive student-centered initiatives like collaboration.

### *Be Creative with Scheduling Collaboration Time*

Scheduling can be one of the trickiest tasks for administrators. Trying to incorporate both the requirements of your state and district as well as the mandates of student IEPs, often threatens the ideal schedule that may best meet all student needs. For special educators who are legally mandated to collaborate, with all staff for the diverse group of students they serve, the dilemma may be all too familiar. With the need to navigate the complexities of both the school schedule demands and what students with IEPs require, special educators can support with the creativity necessary to strategically schedule collaboration time (see Chapter 2). Special educators can assist with considering nontraditional ways of building in collaboration time.

While one of the biggest factors is funding to support such initiatives, being strategic in budgeting at the outset yields greater benefits for both students and staff in the end. Consider building in time on nonstudent days for planned or facilitated collaboration. Yearly, during budget planning, set aside additional money for day-to-day substitutes to ensure one day of collaboration per quarter. Schedule staff lunch during the same time to allow the opportunity to check-in with each other or to schedule a working lunch one or more days a week. You may also set aside funds to pay teachers to come in early or stay late to provide time for collaboration.

### Planning Time

One of the most critical components of collaboration for educators is time to plan. Providing teachers with sufficient time to prepare for collaboration is a major factor that promotes better outcomes. Common and consistent planning time allows for professional dialogue. The best way to grow one's capacity to work with others is to work with others. Embedding a common planning time does not just allow time for staff to build personal relationships and establish common goals, but it also increases the likelihood of improved implementation of selected initiatives. Staff are then able to develop effective plans that should benefit not only students with disabilities, but all students.

### Consider Allowing the Same Team to Loop for Several Years

Another practice that administrators can consider is having teacher teams loop from year to year. Often, special educators work with families over the course of multiple years. Their expertise in practice could aide your school with strategies that make this process successful. With time, staff can foster relationships that nurture professional growth. Looping allows for professional negotiation of routines and practices annually, staff comfort level in working with colleagues improves, making for a dynamic relationship built on respect, understanding, and trust. These characteristics help to build the foundation for lasting professional partnerships.

### Consider Space

Create opportunities for teachers to share space. If teachers are looping together each year, or they will be co-teaching partners, having a shared or common space to work makes planning with a partner simplified. Think about co-teachers who may share a classroom; they may be able to find time throughout their day for co-planning, student analysis, adaptability, etc. As well, common spaces, like a teacher's lounge or workroom, encourage staff collaboration.

### Be a Part of the Problem-Solving Process

Administrators should be part of the collaborative process and model the behaviors of collaboration you seek from your staff. For most change to take effect within schools, the support of administration is key. How an administrator chooses to show support for a promising practice like collaboration can take many shapes. Perhaps collaborating with staff to make schoolwide decisions like selection of a curriculum and truly involving staff in the process or making it a point of being available to support staff through the conflicts of collaborating.

Collaboration must be an integral part of the work taking place within your building. Understanding the who, why, and what to create collaborative relationships gets the process moving. Remember that although an educator or administrator can be a leader in their work, collective planning and support can be an even greater marker for improved student achievement.

---

**STOP AND REFLECT**

1. Who are the key leaders of collaboration within the school community?
2. What is the process for establishing norms and holding team members accountable for meeting them?
3. What is the process for setting goals, communicating about them, and progressing towards them?
4. Do our current time and space structures support effective collaboration amongst staff?
5. How do school leaders model the collaborative process and in what ways can this be communicated with schoolwide staff?

---

## Summary

While some educators remain stagnate in their understanding of collaboration as a means to student success, others embrace this opportunity to improve student outcomes and their school's culture. Establishing collaborative capacity within a school by using the expertise of special educators is paramount to schoolwide collaborative growth. Special educators already possess the skill set necessary to grow a thriving collaborative school community. Through their involvement with school-based IEP team members, schoolwide staff, and the school community at large, they regularly cultivate their collaboration skills. Although co-teaching is not the only way to advance collaboration in your school, it provides a lens from which you may foster collaboration as a way of being in your school. The task to begin this process of collaboration change may not be an easy feat, but by using your special educator's expert knowledge, this process will yield promising results.

## Next Steps

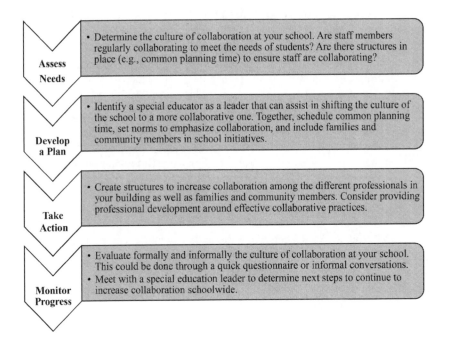

**Assess Needs**
- Determine the culture of collaboration at your school. Are staff members regularly collaborating to meet the needs of students? Are there structures in place (e.g., common planning time) to ensure staff are collaborating?

**Develop a Plan**
- Identify a special educator as a leader that can assist in shifting the culture of the school to a more collaborative one. Together, schedule common planning time, set norms to emphasize collaboration, and include families and community members in school initiatives.

**Take Action**
- Create structures to increase collaboration among the different professionals in your building as well as families and community members. Consider providing professional development around effective collaborative practices.

**Monitor Progress**
- Evaluate formally and informally the culture of collaboration at your school. This could be done through a quick questionnaire or informal conversations.
- Meet with a special education leader to determine next steps to continue to increase collaboration schoolwide.

## References

Buffenbarger, A., Maiers, S., & Rosales, J. (2011, October 11). Partnerships between priority schools and their communities. *NEA Today* http://www.nea.org/archive/47800.htm

Cook, L., & Friend, M. (1991). Principles for the practice of collaboration in schools. *Preventing School Failure: Alternative Education for Children and Youth, 35*(4), 6–9. http://doi.org/10.1080/1045988x.1991.9944251

Cook, S. C., McDuffie-Landrum, K. A., Oshita, L., & Cook, B. G. (2017). Co-Teaching for students with disabilities. In J. M. Kauffman, D. P. Hallahan, & P. C. Pullun (Eds.), *Handbook of special education* (2nd ed., pp. 233–248). Routledge. https://doi.org/10.4324/9781315517698-20

Dieker, L. (n.d.). *Cooperative teaching.* Special Connections. Retrieved, October 31, 2019, from http://www.specialconnections.ku.edu/?q=collaboration/cooperative_teaching

Friend, M., & Cook, L. (1990). Collaboration as a predictor for success in school reform. *Journal of Educational and Psychological Consultation*, *1*(1), 69–86. https://doi.org/10.1207/s1532768xjepc0101_4

Haycock, K. (2007). Collaboration: Critical success factors for student learning. *School Libraries Worldwide*, *13*(1), 25–35.

Hernandez, S. J. (2013). Collaboration in special education: Its history, evolution, and critical factors necessary for successful implementation. *US-China Education Review*, *3*(6), 480–498.

Hoover, J. J., & Teeters, L. (2019). Collaborative decision-making in multicultural contexts. In J.B. Crockett, B. Billingsley, & M. L. Boscardin (Eds.), *Handbook of leadership and administration for special education* (2nd ed., pp. 221–242). Routledge. https://doi.org/10.4324/9781315226378-14.

Individuals with Disabilities Education Act (IDEA), 20 U.S.C. § 1400 (2004).

Pearson, L. C., & Moomaw, W. (2005). The relationship between teacher autonomy and stress, work satisfaction, empowerment, and professionalism. *Educational Research Quarterly*, *29*(1), 38–54.

Pellegrino, A., Weiss, M., & Regan, K. (2015). Learning to collaborate: General and special educators in teacher education. *The Teacher Educator*, *50*(3), 187–202. https://doi.org/10.1080/08878730.2015.1038494

Ronfeldt, M., Farmer, S. O., McQueen, K., & Grissom, J. A. (2015). Teacher collaboration in instructional teams and student achievement. *American Educational Research Journal*, *52* (3), 475–514. https://doi.org/10.3102/0002831215585562

Van Roekel, N. P. D. (2008). Parent, family, community involvement in education. *Policy Brief*. Washington, DC: National education Association. Retrieved from http://www.nea.org/assets/docs/PB11_ParentInvolvement08.pdf

Waldron, N. L., & McLeskey, J. (2010). Establishing a collaborative school culture through comprehensive school reform. *Journal of Educational and Psychological Consultation*, *20*(1), 58–74. https://doi.org/10.1080/10474410903535364

# 8

# ADVOCACY

## Catrina Dorsey and Kary Zarate

Grace is a new special education resource teacher and works with many families who are eager to learn more about how to support their children. While Grace loves working with the families one on one, she wonders if her efforts might be more fruitful if the principal would allow her to sponsor a parent advocacy group to facilitate parent connection, family empowerment, and community collaboration.

| Administrator's perspective | Special educator's perspective |
|---|---|
| Is sponsoring a parent group the best use of our limited time and resources? Aren't there other things our teachers should be doing that can directly impact student learning and raise test scores? Besides, aren't there outside organizations that help families learn how to advocate for their own children? | Supporting families who wish to learn more about helping their children is one of the best ways to increase our impact! By connecting our families with needed resources and supporting their efforts to advocate for their children, we are increasing their capacity to support our learners and enhancing our effectiveness as educators. |

**Key Points:**

- Review the **history** and legacy of advocacy in the field of special education.

- Identify the **six major principles** of special education law.
- Distinguish different **types of advocacy.**
- List shared **competencies** of effective advocates.
- Distinguish the administrator, the general educator, and the special educator's **roles in advocacy.**

## Why Advocacy?

Advocacy is an integral function of the role of a special educator, and it is important that school leaders are aware of the associated ethical, professional, and legal mandates. Just as special educators have a responsibility to support families and students, administrators play an important role in creating a collaborative climate in which special educators are professionally supported in advocacy efforts. Research is clear on the need for school advocacy and its numerous benefits. In many cases, families of children with disabilities enter the school setting hoping to work with school staff as partners in a shared commitment (Zaretsky, 2004). Soon, many of these families encounter multiple systemic barriers. Lack of knowledge (Turnbull & Turnbull, 2003), feelings of intimidation (Fish, 2008), and difficulty interpreting jargon (Park & Turnbull, 2001) have been commonly reported. Some families may find special education regulations perplexing, others have reported feeling unwelcome and having their parental role minimized through attitudinal barriers such as the power differential between schools and families (Leiter & Krauss, 2004). School leaders and educators who position advocacy as a shared community value are likely to eliminate many of these concerns and others. Families and professionals have reported that advocacy can yield positive outcomes for children with disabilities as it may result in teachers being more accountable and children receiving more services (Burke et al., 2019). Families perceive that strong family-school partnerships correlated to a diminished need for outside parent advocacy (Burke et al., 2016), and a reduced need for the most legalistic form of advocacy – due process hearings. Due process is generally filed by families due to disputes regarding educational strategies or supports (Cohen, 2009) and can be laborious and resource intensive for both families and schools. It is of critical importance that families who find themselves at odds with the school about their child's programming have access to resources which can help direct their decision making. One such resource that administrators might provide to families who have questions regarding their legal rights is the Parent Advocacy Center for Educational Rights (PACER). To learn more about this resource, please see Appendix B.

Expectations related to the special educator's role as an advocate are continuously evolving. Evidence of this can be found in the United States legislation of IDEA (2004) as well as in recent revisions to the Every Student

Succeeds Act (ESSA) of 2015, which changed the language of 'parent involvement' to 'parent and family engagement.' This slight but significant change in verbiage signals a shift in focus from the individual parent to community partnership as a whole (Fenton et al., 2017), and places the onus on educators to rethink family involvement and transform the ways in which they invite families to the table for meaningful, productive collaboration.

---

**STOP AND REFLECT**

1. Are there any staff members presently in your building who have strong advocacy skills and are positioned to share those with others?
2. If not, what simple steps can you take to help build capacity for advocacy in your building?

---

Understanding advocacy is important for school leaders because leaders are ultimately charged with supervising the critically complicated and important work of special education teams. When teams do not operate in a manner so that families feel that their children's needs are being met, families with resources may choose to engage the services of advocates outside of the school system. A 2004 study by Zaretsky revealed that though these family advocates and school leaders are often on opposing sides, they both generally agree that schools do not necessarily serve all children equally well. Making advocacy an integral part of the work that schools do on behalf of children and families can greatly enhance the ability of schools to focus on collective change, which can benefit all children (Lalvani & Sauer, 2015).

## Legacy of Advocacy in Special Education

While there are several different contextual definitions, in special education an advocate may be defined as one who supports families in understanding their rights while providing support and guidance through the Individual Education Plan (IEP) process (Goldman et al., 2017). Throughout the history of the United States, advocates have played an enormous role in acquiring and protecting the rights of individuals with disabilities, including helping children in need of special education programming and related services. In the 19th and 20th centuries, many who were concerned about the plight of children with disabilities devoted time and energy to increasing community awareness and working to secure services and protections for these vulnerable citizens. Eventually, these advocates refocused their efforts into issuing formal demands for public institutions to provide educational access, legal protections, and specialized services for children with special needs. It is important to note that prior to this time, public schools in the US had absolutely no legal obligation to meet the special needs of children with disabilities. Some services may have been offered by benevolent groups or charitable individuals responding to an inner moral or ethical imperative, but there was little accountability or oversight, and few assurances that services offered were educational, appropriate, or even meaningful. Few children with serious disabilities had any real chance at being prepared for meaningful participation in society. In the US during the 1960s and 1970s however, advocates for children with disabilities became more vocal in expressing their discontent. Responding, at least in part, to radical social and political shifts ushered in by the American Civil Rights Movement, informal groups of advocates assembled themselves and galvanized into political action, formally petitioning the courts for public access to educational goods and services on behalf of children with disabilities. Once legal protections were secured through the US court system, children's access to a free and appropriate education was legally mandated, and change was imminent. One of the most impactful legislative achievements was the US Individuals with Disabilities Education Act (IDEA), as it was rebranded in the 1990. Key points of this landmark legislation included six major principles that provided children with disabilities the right to (a) a free and appropriate education, (b) an appropriate evaluation, (c) an Individualized Education Plan, (d) receive an education in the least restrictive environment, (e) parental participation in the process, and (f) procedural safeguards. Since the legislation's passage, many of the finer points have been further shaped by reauthorizations, US Supreme Court rulings, and Presidential Acts including the 2001 No Child Left Behind (NCLB) and the 2015 ESSA. However, despite decades of challenges, funding issues, and continuing legal clarifications, advocacy is partially responsible for the fact that the IDEA's six major provisions remain largely intact (see Table 8.1).

If IDEA is to continue to address the increasingly complex needs of children with disabilities in the United States, sustained advocacy must continue to occur at the federal, state, and local levels. In the wake of NCLB and ESSA's calls for greater accountability, many school districts find themselves in the difficult position of being asked to utilize ever dwindling resources to meet ever-increasing demands. In such a climate, educational administrators would be wise to recognize that they have both an opportunity and a responsibility to embrace the role of professional advocacy. Not only should school leaders consider assigning advocacy a prominent position on their own professional agenda, they would do well to also invite special educators to assume key leadership roles in the effort. From the earliest days of the advocacy era, compassionate professionals have partnered with families of children with disabilities. By sharing their valuable professional expertise with families as well as with those who create policy and legislation, special educators have the opportunity

Table 8.1 Six Major Legal Principles of IDEA

| |
|---|
| **FAPE** – Under the law, all students are entitled to receive a Free and Appropriate Public Education which meets their individual needs and prepares them for further education, employment, and individual living. |
| **Appropriate Evaluation** – It is required that evaluations must be conducted by a team of trained evaluators, administered in a nondiscriminatory manner using proper methods and materials, and offered in the child's primary language or mode of communication. |
| **Individualized Education Plan** – Within an established timeline, an IEP must be developed by an IEP team and must incorporate specific information including a student's present levels, goals, and progress. |
| **Least Restrictive Environment** – To the greatest extent possible, a student should be provided with the opportunity to participate in a learning environment with peers in the general education environment. |
| **Parental Participation** – Parents have the right to participate as members of the IEP team. They have rights regarding notification, meetings, evaluation, and the IEP process. |
| **Procedural Safeguards** – Parents' rights in the IEP process include notification timelines for meetings and procedures, review of educational records, and timely notification of their right to request mediation or due process. |

to hone and develop their leadership skills while positively impacting the lives of the children they are committed to serve.

## Special Education Advocacy on Different Levels

In 2000, Dr. Mark Ezell, a professor of social work, proposed a typology to illustrate the different types of advocacy that many nonprofit organizations engage in. In this typology, he distinguished 13 different categories of advocacy, five of which are critically important for special educators: *community, internal, legislative, policy, and political* (see Table 8.2). *Community advocacy* can be as simple as hosting programs to educate and inform the school community about the needs of those with disabilities and taking other simple steps to establish advocacy as a shared value. Special educators and administrators can advocate *internally* by being reflective about their own professional practices and making sure that applicable laws and policies are upheld. *Legislative advocacy* can be facilitated by simply joining and participating in an existing professional organization. *Policy advocacy* is made simpler if relationships are established with those who influence laws, and it should be noted that *all* forms of advocacy might be considered 'political' to some extent since advocacy generally involves working with groups of people who may or may not have shared objectives. Navigating opposing ideas and sorting through complex interpersonal dynamics is crucial for

**Table 8.2** Forms of Advocacy

| Forms of advocacy | Basic description | How administrators and special educators can participate |
|---|---|---|
| Community advocacy | Can include educating and organizing the community as well as challenging assumptions about vulnerable populations | • Raise sensitivity and awareness in the school community<br>• Promote an inclusive and responsive environment |
| Internal advocacy | Working from within an organization to change existing policy, procedure, and practice | • Know requirements of IDEA<br>• Regularly evaluate policies and procedures; identify and remove any barriers |
| Legislative advocacy | Promoting and influencing legislation that will benefit specific populations | • Join and get involved in professional and national organizations that lobby at state and federal levels |
| Policy advocacy | Engaging and influencing those who work to pass legislation, craft public policy, or make court decisions | • Build relationships with local policy makers<br>• Inform and mobilize the community about grassroots efforts |
| Political advocacy | Intervening to influence government policies and practices at the state, local, or federal levels | • Work closely with local officials<br>• Testify at public hearings<br>• Participate in demonstrations, marches, or lobbying |

anyone needing to identify shared goals and accomplish meaningful tasks. An administrator who understands the varied nuances of dealing with the complexities of school politics is far more likely to effectively lead a team of special educator advocates than one who does not.

## Shared Competencies of Effective Advocate Leaders

Although good educators may naturally possess many of the skills and competencies needed to advocate, some have expressed conflicted feelings about picking up the advocacy mantle. Special educators, administrators, and service providers must respond to both the needs of the organization they represent as well as the individual needs of the children they serve, and occasionally, conflicts of interest may arise (Trainor, 2010). Willingness to advocate may also be linked to the professional preferences of the individual. Some special educators and administrators readily embrace advocacy and consider it a natural extension of their job description, while others may not necessarily feel the same. Reluctance to advocate may also be related to confusion attributable to generalized use of the term. In the field of special education, the noun *advocate* is often used to refer to a third-party professional working on behalf of families. These advocates are often viewed as a threat to IEP teams' decisions and might receive a guarded reception from other members of the special education team. In these instances, the advocate is perceived as an adversary. This is unfortunate, because *every* member of a child's IEP team has both an ethical and a legal imperative to advocate on behalf of the child, including the school leader. Advocacy on behalf of children and families with special needs can be a practical way for administrators to take their place within the larger professional community and demonstrate their willingness to work with others seeking to accomplish the same goal: Providing access, opportunities, and services for children with special needs, and sharing resources with the families who love and support them.

---

**STOP AND REFLECT**

All students can benefit from a culture of shared advocacy – not just those who qualify for services under IDEA. School leaders can encourage special educators in leadership positions to use their unique perspectives, skills, and specialized training to improve access for students throughout the entire school community.

How can you empower your special educators to share more of their skills with the entire school population?

---

Although the functional roles of school administrators and professional special education advocates might be regarded quite differently, the two roles actually share a common set of professional skills and competencies. For example, both must be skilled in data analysis and need to have more than a basic understanding of current and emerging trends in research and policy. Both must be resourceful, need a foundational understanding of relevant laws and procedures, and must be able to exercise sound communication skills in the dispatch of their professional duties. Shields (1987) identified foundational knowledge, competencies, and dispositions that all effective advocates need (see Figure 8.1). However, it might be argued that school administrators and special educators need to possess *additional* advocacy

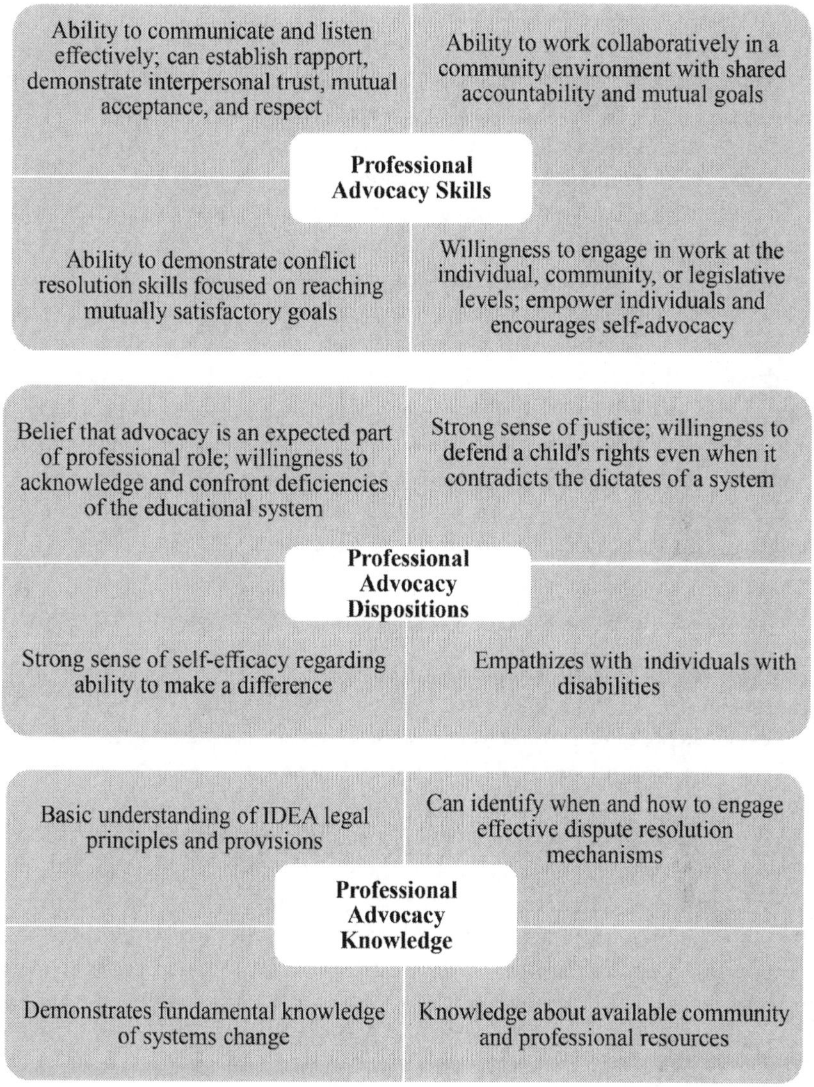

Ability to communicate and listen effectively; can establish rapport, demonstrate interpersonal trust, mutual acceptance, and respect

Ability to work collaboratively in a community environment with shared accountability and mutual goals

**Professional Advocacy Skills**

Ability to demonstrate conflict resolution skills focused on reaching mutually satisfactory goals

Willingness to engage in work at the individual, community, or legislative levels; empower individuals and encourages self-advocacy

Belief that advocacy is an expected part of professional role; willingness to acknowledge and confront deficiencies of the educational system

Strong sense of justice; willingness to defend a child's rights even when it contradicts the dictates of a system

**Professional Advocacy Dispositions**

Strong sense of self-efficacy regarding ability to make a difference

Empathizes with individuals with disabilities

Basic understanding of IDEA legal principles and provisions

Can identify when and how to engage effective dispute resolution mechanisms

**Professional Advocacy Knowledge**

Demonstrates fundamental knowledge of systems change

Knowledge about available community and professional resources

Adapted from Fiedler & Clark, 2009, p. 21-23; Shields, 1987

**Figure 8.1** Key Professional Advocacy Competencies.

dispositions, knowledge, and skills. Special education leaders must know how to work effectively with others in pursuit of shared goals and mutually agreeable outcomes that benefit vulnerable children and their families. They also need to be reflective and understand that responsible advocacy demands reflection and accountability, not just calls for change. Finally, educational leaders who advocate have to acknowledge that advocacy requires follow-through when new ideas are implemented and must demonstrate a willingness to be flexible when appropriate adjustments need to be made. Good advocates on any level also must be careful to guard their credibility. They understand that they will not be taken seriously if their advocacy efforts are not perceived as ethical and well-informed.

Another way that special educators and administrators differ from other professional advocates is that they focus most of their efforts within the school setting *implementing* emerging trends, while other types of advocates may focus most of their efforts outside of the school setting *influencing* such trends. This distinction is key. Prudent educational administrators understand that the internal policies they supervise and evaluate are largely influenced by forces beyond the school walls. Thus, engaging in professional advocacy on behalf of students in external settings not only benefits students and families, it also serves to ensure that administrators themselves are positioned to provide informed input on the policies that will shape and influence the future of the field of special education.

## School Leaders Supporting a Climate and Culture of Advocacy

As educators and school leaders advocate for students, they share a common responsibility to help provide students with disabilities the services and experiences they are entitled to in accordance with the stated aims and mission of laws and policies already in place. Though some school administrators may be understandably reluctant to invest the time and energy necessary to engage at higher levels of advocacy, it should be noted that opportunities abound to engage in meaningful advocacy at the local, organizational, and community levels. In schools, administrators can easily promote sensitivity and awareness by implementing informative school programming that empowers impacted families with needed tools and resources, while raising awareness within the larger school community. Advocating administrators who wish to get involved at the legislative, policy, and political levels on broader issues such as equalized funding or school budgets can easily do so by joining forces with outside organizations already working on those topics.

The point is that *effective administrative advocacy need not be complicated, overwhelming, or time consuming!* When advocacy is positioned as a shared responsibility and embedded within organizational climate and culture, administrators can easily share the workload with knowledgeable special educators, general educators, and families. Administrators can facilitate advocacy in the entire school community by:

- Establishing a rotation for attending and participating in local school board meetings.

- Signing the school up for email alerts from external advocacy agencies.
- Meeting regularly with a multidisciplinary team to review, identify, and monitor school policies which may unduly impact children with special needs.
- Publicizing important issues in the form of announcements, website links, or press releases to the larger school community.

Administrators can also support special educators and staff in their individual and collective efforts to professionally advocate for themselves and for their students. Administrators should recognize the importance of establishing a safe environment in which all teachers are respected as skilled professionals, are free to ask appropriate questions, and can respectfully challenge existing policies and practices without fear of professional reprisal. General educators, who may or may not have much foundational knowledge about special education, are on the front line working with the majority of the student body and are often among the first to notice that a child might need to be considered for specialized services. Administrators have a responsibility to establish and maintain appropriate screening and identification systems that will enable general educators to make sound and knowledgeable recommendations. School administrators can also encourage general educators to participate in advocacy efforts by bringing in relevant professional development that the entire school community can participate in and benefit from. Efforts toward establishing more inclusive learning environments will be far more effective when general educators are provided with training that inculcates the desired dispositions necessary to maintaining a climate of advocacy (see Chapter 2). When administrators take the opportunity to invite general educators to the table, it helps to ensure that the entire school community has a shared vision that everyone can work toward and meaningfully contribute to. Both the Arc and Learning Disabilities Association of America are resources provided in Appendix B where administrators can look for relevant resources to assist in this important effort.

Special educators have specific ways in which they typically advocate for their students. It may be useful for administrators to consider that when working on behalf of their students, a special educator's advocacy efforts may generally fall into one or more of the following three basic categories:

- **Obtaining** resources for students that might not be provided otherwise. Such resources might come from either inside or outside the school setting and may include either goods or services. Administrators can support these advocacy efforts by helping to ensure that needed resources are available to the teachers, or by supporting teachers' efforts to secure needed materials from other sources.

- **Modifying** assignments, practices, procedures, or policies as appropriate given the parameters of the child's IEP. Administrators can support these advocacy efforts by establishing the expectation that general educators will support special educators' attempts to minimize and reduce barriers to equal access.
- **Promoting** new policies or legislation that may increase access to services or resources for needy student populations. Administrators can support advocacy efforts of this type by staying abreast of evolving legislation, and by getting involved in community organizations that are already active in policy work.

---

**STOP AND REFLECT**

Engaged families are among the most valuable resources in a school community.

1. How does your school actively support family advocacy?
2. What steps can you take to either establish a new family advocate group in your school or to improve the family advocacy group that you already have?

---

Like administrators, special educators should also be encouraged to consider the wisdom of advocating at different levels both within and beyond school settings. In schools, special educators best represent the needs of their students by empowering families, promoting inclusive environments, ensuring that IEPs are being followed, and advocating knowledgeably in IEP meetings. To inform and support their in-school efforts, teacher advocates will need to look outside of the school setting for guidance and resources. Reading professional journals and following relevant news stories at the federal, state, and local levels are important ways of keeping up with current and emerging trends. Joining local and national professional organizations is an effective way to make professional contacts and to gain access to information and useful resources. While much can be learned from simply reviewing publications, involvement at the committee level of local, state, and national organizations can also offer expanded professional networking opportunities that build awareness, increase professional knowledge, and provide enhanced access to digital resources such as newsletters, webcasts, or podcasts.

## Supporting Family Advocates

In addition to the teaching staff, administrators can also help support family advocacy efforts in practical ways. For families, educational advocacy is perhaps the most important way they can be educated about and empowered to secure necessary goods and services for their child with a disability. Special education can be a maze for families due to the myriad emotions that come along with raising a child with disabilities, the bewildering legalities of special education law, and the dizzying array of acronyms routinely tossed around IEP tables. The innate complexity and constantly evolving nature of the field of special education makes it vital that families have meaningful opportunities to plug into groups and make connections with others who are knowledgeable about and know how to find necessary resources. To learn more about resources to encourage family advocacy see resources from the Council for Exceptional Children in Appendix B.

Advocacy can be difficult for any family of a child with a disability, it can be particularly difficult for those who have neither the knowledge nor the means to access help-for-hire. Families often turn to outside advocates when they have concerns about the school meeting their child's needs, but when schools elect to actively support advocacy, home/school bonds can be strengthened. Compassionate and knowledgeable school professionals are a logical and convenient source of information for families when questions about services or programming arise. When school professionals provide space and support for families to advocate, it can help level the playing field for under-resourced families by offering them tools, access, knowledge, or services they might not otherwise have been privy to.

Establishing a school supported family group is one way that administrators and special educators can meaningfully support all families' efforts to empower themselves while simultaneously demonstrating a willingness to work together in the context of a mutually respectful learning space. By inviting families into a collaborative workspace for the benefit of students, administrators can openly and authentically demonstrate their professional advocacy dispositions, skills, and knowledge while also providing families with a forum to voice their questions and concerns. With very little effort, even school leaders who are unwilling to fully commit to advocacy may support parental advocacy. Special educators on staff can be commissioned to pick up the leadership mantle by:

- **Hosting guest speakers who can present on relevant topics** – Engaging the services of professionals who work outside of the district can help both families and the district stay current with special education issues and concerns. Some of these professionals may even be willing to donate their time and services. The entire school community can benefit from the knowledge that is shared.
- **Creating spaces and events which encourage families to support and share knowledge with one another** – Providing families with opportunities to learn from one another is a powerful way to promote

self-advocacy, establish a collaborative environment, and help families form and nurture supportive partnerships among themselves.

- **Allowing district personnel to make professional presentations** – Giving educators and related service providers time and opportunities to share their professional expertise can increase families' understanding of how these various professionals serve their children and can allow families to benefit from their highly specialized knowledge. Allowing staff to make these presentations at regularly scheduled school events such as open houses and curriculum nights would prevent staff from having to work extra hours.
- **Connecting families with community resources** – There are many local, state, and national groups who make it their full-time mission to help individuals with disabilities. Schools can establish partnerships with these groups and build bridges between those organizations and families, which can greatly benefit the entire school community. Each state in the US has a parent training and information program (PTI) which is federally funded and set up to support families in their advocacy efforts. Schools may consider reaching out to these PTIs and finding out ways to bring featured resources directly into the school for families who may not have direct access to the PTI. Interested families can use the resources at the PTI to learn about available resources, programs, and services and to find tips on effective communication and participation in the educational planning process.
- **Hosting family/professional book clubs** – one of the easiest ways to get families involved is to select an appropriate book, start a book club, and invite families to join in. Snacks and childcare can be provided, and the book selections can follow families expressed topics of interest.

Administrators might find that supporting and encouraging teachers and families to assume a mantle of advocacy may actually prove to be a protective factor for a school or district. When teachers and families are engaged in a mutually respectful and collaborative setting, they are more likely to share issues or concerns that school leaders need to be made aware of. When general educators are invited to participate in advocacy activities, their overall knowledge of special education laws and policies is likely to significantly increase, lessening the likelihood that they will engage in actions that may violate certain principles. When special educators are encouraged to share their specialized skills and knowledge with the larger school community in support of advocacy efforts, all children get to benefit from their wealth of wisdom and training (see Chapter 2). As the culture and climate of the school changes, reduced teacher turnover and increased organizational efficiency are likely to be observed. School leaders may have an opportunity to proactively address any potential issues or concerns that do arise with minimal conflict or escalation. For administrators who remain nervous about committing scarce time and energy resources to advocacy, it should be noted that administrative support for general and special educator advocacy may be either tacit or explicit in nature. Opportunities may be as simple as asking teachers to:

- Participate in building- and district-level committees.
- Collaborate on projects and initiatives that promote tolerance and inclusivity.
- Attend, participate in, and possibly even present at district functions such as parent-teacher conferences, school board meetings, and committee meetings to represent their interests and make their voices heard.

## Supporting Student Advocates

No discussion of special education advocacy would be complete without acknowledging the need for teaching age appropriate self-advocacy skills to students with disabilities. The development of self-advocacy is critical for those who live with disabilities, and school is the ideal setting in which to introduce and nurture this necessary life skill. It is important that students with disabilities learn their rights and are taught effective ways to assert themselves appropriately across social settings. Special educators can be commissioned to work with building-level team members to support student advocates by encouraging age-appropriate participation in decision making and IEP development. Special educators can also take the lead on working with building-level team members to establish age-appropriate policies and procedures that prioritize equipping student learners with the tools they will need to advocate for themselves throughout their lives and across social settings.

## Summary

We recognize that educational leaders are uniquely positioned to coordinate and facilitate advocacy efforts for their organizational stakeholders. By positioning advocacy as a shared value and a shared responsibility, advocate administrators can indicate their willingness to work to uphold the rights of students with disabilities in a sustainable way. When school administrators offer special educators the opportunity to share their knowledge and utilize their training beyond the classroom setting, it can benefit all students, not only those who are protected by specific laws and policies. All teachers have the capacity to lead, and when administrators make it a point to strategically engage teachers to the fullness of their professional potential, everyone in the school community can reap the rewards.

There is no question that advocacy takes dedication, time, and effort. The critical importance of the mission dictates no less, but the burdens of the workload can easily be shared. Advocacy, situated as an integral component of organizational climate and culture, builds on the rich historical tradition of special education advocacy and must be practiced with due deliberation and skill. Children with disabilities are among the least powerful and most vulnerable in our society and all educators have an ethical and professional obligation to invest time and energy elevating their cause. In this manner, our work continues toward the aim and mission of IDEA being fully realized in the lives of the students and families it was designed to protect. The services and benefits currently available under IDEA were once just the collective vision of a dedicated army of advocates who tirelessly fought for them to become reality. Individuals with differences and disabilities have access to the many services they utilize today due to the power of advocacy.

School leaders have the responsibility to establish advocacy as both a shared value and a shared responsibility, *but they need not do so alone!* There are many resources in the community-individuals and entities alike – who work on behalf of individuals with disabilities and who can offer the benefit of their expertise to school leaders who wish to support their stakeholders in this all-important task. Simply stated, advocacy is important work because advocates change things. Advocates work to change hearts and minds and in doing so they change practices and laws. Advocates work to change culture and climate, and in doing so, they increase tolerance and respect.

Advocacy is not just a hobby or a professional pastime. For educators, advocacy is a shared professional responsibility. School administrators should welcome opportunities to speak truth to those with power to craft the policies, procedures, and practices that school staff are asked to implement. Special educators, by virtue of their personal calling and their professional training, are uniquely qualified to step into prepared spaces and share specialized knowledge with the entire school community. General educators also have an important role to play and should be offered professional development to assist in making instructional and disciplinary decisions that promote educational equity and cultural responsivity. When school administrators, special educators, and general educators each understand and embrace their unique roles as advocates, the entire school community can reap the benefits of having advocacy positioned as an integral component of the organizational culture and climate.

## Next Steps

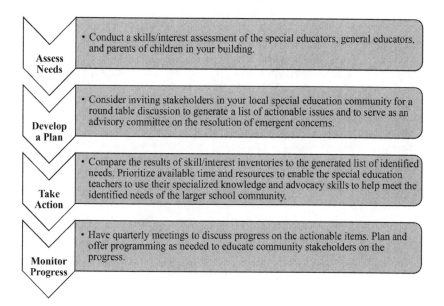

**Assess Needs**
- Conduct a skills/interest assessment of the special educators, general educators, and parents of children in your building.

**Develop a Plan**
- Consider inviting stakeholders in your local special education community for a round table discussion to generate a list of actionable issues and to serve as an advisory committee on the resolution of emergent concerns.

**Take Action**
- Compare the results of skill/interest inventories to the generated list of identified needs. Prioritize available time and resources to enable the special education teachers to use their specialized knowledge and advocacy skills to help meet the identified needs of the larger school community.

**Monitor Progress**
- Have quarterly meetings to discuss progress on the actionable items. Plan and offer programming as needed to educate community stakeholders on the progress.

## References

Burke, M. M., Goldman, S., Hart, M. S., & Hodapp, M. (2016). Evaluating the efficacy of a special education advocacy training program. *Journal of Policy and Practice in Intellectual Disabilities, 13*(4), 269–276. https://doi.org/10.1111/jppi.12183

Burke, M. M., Rios, K., & Lee, C. (2019). Exploring the special education advocacy process according to families and advocates. *The Journal of Special Education, 53*(3), 131–141. https://doi.org/10.1177/0022466918810204

Cohen, M. (2009). *A guide to special education advocacy.* Jessica Kingsley Publishers.

Ezell, M. (2000). *Advocacy in the human services.* Cengage Learning.

Fenton, P., Ocasio-Stoutenburg, L., & Harry, B. (2017). The power of parent engagement: Sociocultural considerations in the quest for equity. *Theory into Practice, 56*(3), 214–225. https://doi.org/10.1080/00405841.2017.1355686

Fish, W. W. (2008). The IEP meeting: Perceptions of parents of students who receive special education services. *Preventing School Failure: Alternative Education for Children and Youth, 53*(1), 8–14. https://doi.org/10.3200/psfl.53.1.8-14

Goldman, S. E., Burke, M. M., Mason, C. Q., & Hodapp, R. M. (2017). Correlates of sustained volunteering: Advocacy for students with disabilities. *Exceptionality, 25*(1), 40–53. https://doi.org/10.1080/09362835.2015.1064420

Lalvani, P., & Sauer, J. (2015). *From advocacy to activism: Families, inclusive education and radical change* [Presentation]. Society for Disability Studies, Atlanta, GA.

Leiter, V., & Krauss, M. (2004). Claims, barriers, and satisfaction: Parents' requests for additional special education services. *Journal of Disability Policy Studies, 15*(3), 135–146. https://doi.org/10.1177/10442073040150030201

Park, J., & Turnbull, A. P. (2001). Quality of partnerships in service provision for Korean American parents of children with disabilities: A qualitative inquiry. *Research and Practice for Persons with Severe Disabilities, 26*(3), 158–170. https://doi.org/10.2511/rpsd.26.3.158

Shields, C. V. (1987). *Strategies: A practical guide for dealing with professionals and human service systems.* Human Services Press.

Trainor, A. A. (2010). Diverse approaches to parent advocacy during special education home—School interactions: Identification and use of cultural and social capital. *Remedial and Special Education, 31*(1), 34–47. https://doi.org/10.1177/0741932508324401

Turnbull, R., & Turnbull, A. P. (2003). Reaching the ideal. *Education Next, 3*, 32–37. https://www.educationnext.org/files/ednext20031_32.pdf

Zaretsky, L. (2004). Responding ethically to complex school-based issues in special education. *International Studies in Educational Administration, 32*(2), 63–77.

# APPENDIX A

## Special Education Resources

## Amanda Passmore and Geraldo Tobon

Appendix A is intended to supply leaders with an initial overview of special education principles and practices. Sections will also outline additional web and print resources to direct you to more information on these topics.

### Legal Requirements of Special Education

Special education services in public schools and students with disabilities are protected by various procedural safeguards and federal laws. These legal requirements are outlined in the American's with Disabilities Act (ADA), Section 504 of the 1973 Vocational Rehabilitation Act, and the Individuals with Disabilities Act (IDEA).

### *Section 504*

- Civil rights law that protects individuals with disabilities from discrimination in programs receiving federal funding.

- Plan of how schools will provide support and remove barriers for students with disabilities.
- Provides students with reasonable accommodations that will support their needs in the school environment.

### Americans with Disabilities Act (ADA)

- Civil rights law that prohibits discrimination of people with disabilities by schools, employers, and anyone who provides goods and services to the public.
- States that people with disabilities have the right to reasonable accommodations so they can have the same access to various aspects of everyday life.
- Accommodations are not required if it causes an undue burden or a fundamental alteration to what is being offered by the school, program, or business.

### Individuals with Disabilities Act (IDEA)

- Special education law for children with disabilities.
- Federal funded law that provides aid to states to provide children with disabilities a free appropriate public education (FAPE).
- Outlines how students found eligible for special education based on having one or more of the 13 disabilities listed in IDEA are provided with special education and related services.
- States that students are to be educated in the Least Restrictive Environment (LRE).

### Website Resources

#### Office of Special Education Programing (OSEP)

One of the resources, the OSEP website, offers educators an overview of special education legislation, regulations, and other policy documentations. A link to these resources is found on their homepage.
www.2.ed.gov/

#### Wrights Law

Wrights law provides information about special education law, education law, and advocacy for students with disabilities in user-friendly language. Wrights law also provides several additional publications, newsletters, and resources on these topics.
www.wrightslaw.com/

*The Individuals with Disabilities Act (IDEA) Disability Categories*

IDEA requires that public schools provide special education and related services to students identified with a disability in one or more of the 13 disability categories. Student performance must be 'adversely affected' in one or more of the 13 disability categories: Specific Learning Disability (SLD), Other Health Impairment (OHI), Autism Spectrum Disorder (ASD), Emotional Disturbance (ED), Speech and Language Impairment (SLI), Visual Impairment, including blindness, Deafness, Hearing Impairment (HI), Deaf-Blindness, Orthopedic Impairment, Intellectual Disability (ID), Traumatic Brain Injury (TBI), Multiple Disabilities.
https://www.understood.org/en/school-learning/special-services/
special-education-basics/conditions-covered-under-idea

### Print Resources

*Your Classroom Guide to Special Education Law by B. H. Johns (2016)*

Johns provides an interactive quick look into special education law and its influence on classroom practices by providing reader-friendly definitions and descriptions of federal law. The text is geared toward both administrators and teachers.

*A Principal's Guide to Special Education by David
F. Bateman and C. Fred Bateman (2014)*

Through this text, guidance is provided to administrators on meeting the needs of students with disabilities at their school. The authors provide insights to a principal's role in placement, accountability, and legal requirements.

### Special Education Terminology

Special education and the provided services are associated with various terminologies. Table A.1 outlines some common terms used in special education.

### Print Resources

*What Every Principal Needs to Know About Special Education
(2nd Ed.) by Margaret J. McLaughlin (2009)*

McLaughlin provides an overview of special education policies and practices to ensure administrators are supporting students with disabilities in reaching their full potential through high-quality special education services.

**Table A.1** Common Special Education Terms

| | |
|---|---|
| **Accommodation** | Accommodations are a change to or in a student's learning environment that are intended to offset the impact of that student's disability. Accommodations can help students learn and allows students to show what they learned without having challenges presented, as part of their disability, get in the way. An accommodation can be a device or learning support. Common accommodations involve extended time, visual supports, or receiving directions orally. It is important to note that even with accommodations, students are expected to access the same content as their peers. |
| **Annual goals** | The Individual Education Program (IEP) document lists the academic and functional skills the IEP team thinks a student can achieve by the end of the year. These goals need to be specific, measurable, attainable, and geared toward helping students access the general education classroom. |
| **Assistive technology (AT)** | Any device, tool, piece of equipment, or software that helps a student is considered assistive technology (AT). Provided AT can help a student learn, communicate, and function better in school. AT ranges from simple tools (highlighters) to high-tech software (communication device). |
| **Behavior intervention plan (BIP)** | A BIP is a comprehensive plan aimed to address the causes and consequences of a specific problem behavior. The plan is designed to teach and reinforce a specific positive replacement behavior. Typically, the plan uses preventive strategies to stop problem behaviors as opposed to being reactive to behaviors. A BIP may also outline supports and aids for the student's behaviors. A child must first have a functional behavior assessment (FBA) before an IEP team begins a BIP. |
| **Due process** | A formal process for families seeking to resolve disputes with a school about special education and IEP. |
| **Extended school year services (ESY)** | Extended school year refers to students who receive special education services outside of the regular school year, such as during the summer. ESY services can also be provided during winter break, but this is less common. The purpose for ESY is to combat any regression in academic or functional progress. |

(Continued)

**Table A.1** Common Special Education Terms (*Continued*)

| | |
|---|---|
| **Free and appropriate education (FAPE)** | Children with disabilities – including eligible learning and attention issues – have the right to FAPE. FAPE is the basic legal entitlement of students identified with a disability. The term *appropriate* is in relation to the IEP. FAPE ensures that students with disabilities receive an education that is *appropriate* and meets their individual needs. |
| **Functional behavior assessment (FBA)** | An FBA is an approach to problem behavior that is required under IDEA. It is used to determine the root of a student's behavioral problems by seeking to uncover correlations or causes related to a specific behavior. Done through identifying social, emotional, and environmental causes, following the FBA a school writes a BIP, which outlines how to address the issues uncovered in the FBA process. |
| **Individualized education program (IEP)** | An IEP is a legally binding document that is specific for each student with a qualifying disability. The IEP holds a school accountable for providing educational services that enable a student to progress through their grade-level curriculum. An IEP is a personalized plan that directs a student's education by outlining educational goals, academic challenges, and strengths by describing how a student currently doing academically and functioning in the school environment. An IEP also lists when and where a student will receive special education services and accommodations. The IEP is developed using a team approach that consist of a general education teacher, special education teacher, service providers, and families. |
| **Least restrictive environment (LRE)** | Students with documented disabilities must be taught in the LRE. LRE means students are to be taught in the same setting as students without documented disabilities for as much of the school day as possible. LRE is a requirement of IDEA and is measured in terms of percentage of time that a student with a disability is educated outside the general education classroom. The school must offer services and supports to help a student with an IEP succeed in a general education classroom. |
| **Modification** | A modification is a change to what a student is expected to learn and demonstrate. Modifications can be an adjustment made to curriculum or assessment. These adjustments alter the level of performance expected from a student. Modifications should be outlined in a student's IEP. |

(*Continued*)

**Table A.1** Common Special Education Terms (*Continued*)

| | |
|---|---|
| **Progress reporting (IEP report card)** | How a school will report to families a student's progress on annual goals outlined in their IEP. |
| **Present level of performance (PLOP, PLP, PLAFF, PLAAFP)** | The PLOP section of an IEP is a snapshot of how a student is doing currently. PLOP describes a student's academic skills (such as reading level) and functional skills (such as making conversation or writing with a pencil). PLOP is the starting point for setting annual IEP goals and identifying what supports a student may need to be successful toward meeting these goals. |
| **Supplementary aids and services** | These are supports to help a student learn in the general education classroom. They can include equipment or assistive technology, like audiobooks or highlighted classroom notes. They may also include training for staff. |
| **Related services** | Any support services a student may need to benefit from special education. Examples include transportation, speech, and occupational therapy. |
| **Transition plan** | Transition planning is outlined in a student's IEP and lays out what students must learn and do in high school in order to succeed as a young adult. The IEP team develops the plan together before it initiates at age 16. The transition plan includes goals and activities that are academic and functional. Transition planning can also be done at the preschool level to support students moving into kindergarten and the elementary setting. |

Bateman and Cline (2016), McLaughlin (2009); adapted from http:understood.org.

## Abbreviations in Special Education

There is a plethora of terminology related to special education policies, procedures, and practices. Abbreviations and jargon are commonly used among special education service providers. The following section outlines some of the common abbreviations used in the field.

**ADA**   Americans with Disabilities Act (1990)
**ADD**   Attention deficit disorder
**ADHD**  Attention deficit hyperactivity disorder
**ASD**   Autism spectrum disorder
**AT**    Assistive technology

| | |
|---|---|
| **BD** | Behavior, or behavioral disorder |
| **BIP** | Behavior intervention plan |
| **CBA** | Curriculum-based assessment |
| **CBM** | Curriculum-based measurement |
| **CD** | Communication disorder |
| **DBI** | Data-based individualization |
| **DD** | Developmental delay |
| **DSM-5** | Diagnostic and Statistical Manual of Mental Disorders, 5th Edition |
| **EBP** | Evidence-based practice |
| **ED** | Emotional disturbance |
| **EI** | Early intervention |
| **ELL** | English language learner; also called EL, for English learner |
| **ESY** | Extended school year |
| **FAPE** | Free appropriate public education |
| **FBA** | Functional behavior assessment |
| **GLE** | Grade-level equivalent or grade-level expectations |
| **HI** | Hearing impairment |
| **ID** | Intellectual disability |
| **IDEA** | Individuals with Disabilities Education Act |
| **IEP** | Individual education program |
| **IFSP** | Individual family service plan, for students 3 or younger |
| **IQ** | Intelligence quotient |
| **ITP** | Individual transition plan |
| **IWRP** | Individualized written rehabilitation plan |
| **LD** | Learning disability |
| **LRE** | Least restrictive environment |
| **MA** | Mental age |
| **MDE** | Multidisciplinary evaluation |
| **MDT** | Multidisciplinary team |
| **MTSS** | Multitiered system of support |
| **NVLD** | Nonverbal learning disabilities |
| **ODD** | Oppositional defiant disorder |
| **OHI** | Other health impairment |
| **OT** | Occupational therapy |
| **PBIS** | Positive behavioral interventions and supports |
| **PDD** | Pervasive developmental disorder |
| **PLAAFP** | Present levels of academic achievement and functional performance |
| **PLEP** | Present levels of educational performance |
| **PT** | Physical therapy |
| **PWN** | Prior written notice |

| RTI | Response to intervention |
|-----|--------------------------|
| SDI | Specially designed instruction |
| SEA | State education agency |
| SLP | Speech language pathologist |
| TBI | Traumatic brain injury |
| UDL | Universally designed instruction |

## Website Resources

### US Department of Education: Individuals with Disabilities Education Act (IDEA)

Overview of acronyms, abbreviations, and terms associated with the Individuals with Disabilities Education Act (IDEA). Acronyms, abbreviations, and terms are organized alphabetically for easy reference.
https://sites.ed.gov/idea/acronyms/

### Center for Parent Information and Resources

Overview of 13 disability categories covered within the Individual with Disabilities Education Act (IDEA). Resources are available in both English and Spanish.
https://www.parentcenterhub.org/categories/

## Individualized Education Program (IEP) Process

The special education process is one of the hallmarks of special education. Through this process, different professionals come together to create an individualized education program (IEP) for students with disabilities. The process begins with a referral made by a staff member or a parent (see Figure A.1). Depending on the school's response, the student receives an educational evaluation. Following the evaluation, an eligibility meeting takes places where the results are analyzed to determine whether the student qualified for special education services under one of the disability categories. Next, an IEP is created. Student progress is discussed yearly and the IEP is updated with new goals, accommodations, and modifications. Every 3 years, an evaluation takes place to determine continued eligibility. Administrators are tasked with making sure all students with an IEP are provided with the necessary services as written in their individual plans. Administrators should also be prepared to lead meetings; therefore, they must be well versed with the IEP process. Administrators should also be familiar with all students and be prepared to talk about them in meetings.

| | |
|---|---|
| **Referral** | • Parent or staff initiates a referral based on concerns.<br>• School decides whether to pursue an educational evaluation.<br>• Prior to referral, school must demonstrate that tiered interventions were attempted. |
| **Educational Evaluation** | • Various school professionals, including the school psychologist, will give the student appropriate evaluations.<br>• Student records will be reviewed and the child will be observed in his or her classroom. |
| **Eligibility Determination** | • Based on the evaluation results, the child is either found eligible or ineligible for special education services.<br>• In order to be eligible, the evaluation report needs to show that the child has a disability and this disability negatively impacts the child's learning. |
| **Initial IEP Meeting** | • An IEP meeting is held to discuss goals, accommodations, modifications, and placement.<br>• Families must agree to the IEP and any changes made after this meeting must be brought to the family for approval. |
| **Annual IEP Meeting** | • A yearly IEP meeting is held to discuss student progress and create new goals. |
| **Triannual Evaluation** | • Every three years the child is reevaluated to determine whether the child continues to be eligible for special education services. |

**Figure A.1** IEP Process.

## School Professionals Who Work with Students with IEPs

Below is a list of professionals who might work with a student with disabilities. The type of services a child receives depends on the child's disability and how their disability negatively impacts their learning.

**School psychologist:** Completes a full assessment to determine eligibility.

**General education teacher:** Discuss students functioning in the general education classroom.

**Special education teacher:** Provide specialized instruction based on student needs.

**Speech language pathologist:** Provide services based on students' difficulties with speech and language.

**Social worker:** Provides students with services in helping them manage emotions, make positive choices, and navigating relationships.

**Occupational therapist:** Addresses physical, cognitive, and sensory needs.

**Vision and mobility specialist:** Provides services for students who are visually impaired.

**Physical therapist:** Provides services for students with physical disabilities.

**Audiologist:** Provides services for students who are deaf or hard of hearing.

**Paraprofessionals:** Provides support to students with academics, daily living, or medical needs.

## Website Resources

### Innovative Resources or Instructional Success (IRIS) Center: Developing High-Quality IEPs

This module provides information on how to develop high-quality IEPs for students with disabilities that meet all legal requirements.
https://iris.peabody.vanderbilt.edu/module/iep01/

### Innovative Resources or Instructional Success (IRIS) Center: The Prereferral Process

This module describes the prereferral process which can help eliminate inappropriate referrals to special education.
https://iris.peabody.vanderbilt.edu/module/preref/

## Print Resources

### Supporting the IEP Process: A Facilitators Guide by Nicholas R. M. Martin (2010)

This guide provides facilitators with practical tools and strategies for how to facilitate IEP meetings effectively. The guide also provides useful tips on how to navigate difficult situations that arise during IEP meetings.

## Instruction in Special Education

Instruction in special education may look different then instruction for general education students. Instruction for students with disabilities needs to be intentional and individualized. There are various strategies and frameworks used to ensure that all students are learning. Further, instruction for students with disabilities needs to have a strong evidence for effectiveness in research.

## Website Resources

### National Professional Development Center on Autism Spectrum Disorder (NPDC)

The NPDC provides educators with evidence-based practices for use with students with autism spectrum disorder.
https://autismpdc.fpg.unc.edu/

### Best Evidence Encyclopedia (BEE): National Professional Development Center on Autism Spectrum Disorder

The BEE website provides educational professionals with information regarding the strength of evidence for a variety of academic programs including reading, mathematics, and writing.
http://www.bestevidence.org/

### Florida Center for Reading Research (FCRR)

The FCRR provides practitioners with a variety of resources for effective reading instruction for all students.
https://www.fcrr.org/

## Print Resources

### High Leverage Practices in Special Education by Council for Exceptional Children & CEEDAR Center (2017)

This book describes the practices and activities that all special educators need to implement in order to provide students with disabilities a high-quality education.

### High Leverage Practices for Inclusive Classrooms by James McLeskey, Lawrence Maheady, Boonie Billingsley, Mary T. Brownell, & Timothy J. Lewis (2019)

This book provides practical information around an important set of practices that both special education and general education teachers must know to support students with mild disabilities in general education.

## Assessment in Special Education

Data collection and analysis are essential components in special education. Special education teachers routinely give students a variety of assessments to determine progress with IEP goals and to pinpoint areas of need. Students who are included in general education are expected to demonstrate their learning of classroom content through classroom, state/national, and district standardized assessments, respectively. In order for children to access these tests, they might require accommodations. Accommodations change how a student takes a test; they are held to the same expectations as all students. Sometimes, a child is far below grade level that he or she might need modifications. Modifications changes what a child is tested on. To avoid setting low expectations, modifications to an assessment should be done only when necessary. See Table A.2 for common testing accommodations and modifications.

### Website Resources

### National Center of Educational Outcomes (NCEO)

NCEO provides technical assistance with assessment of students with disabilities, English learners, and English learners with disabilities. The site provides resources on how to use assessment to make instructional decisions. https://nceo.info/

### Intervention Central

Provides users with tools and resources around academic and behavioral interventions. Intervention Central contains a feature where users can create curriculum-based measures to help them monitor progress of interventions being implemented and to help them inform their instruction. https://www.interventioncentral.org/teaching-resources/downloads

### Easy CBM

Easy CBM is a website and program containing curriculum-based measures of different areas of reading and math. These measures are meant to be used to track the effectiveness of interventions as well as to make instructional decisions based on data. https://www.easycbm.com/

## Behavioral Supports for Special Education

Students with a disability should be accountable to the same school rules and expectations as their typically developing peers. However, students with an Individual Education Program (IEP) will follow different

**Table A.2** Testing Accommodations

| Extended time | Provide more time for a child who requires additional time to process information. |
|---|---|
| Small group | Allow student to take the test in a small group to allow them to focus. |
| Separate location | A separate location helps students who are easily distracted in the general education classroom. |
| One-on-one testing | This accommodation is used for students who are severely distracted or for students with severe behavior needs. |
| Breaks | Breaks are provided to students who have a difficult time sustaining their attention for a long period of time. |
| Take the test during multiple sessions | For students that have a difficult time sustaining their attention despite given breaks, allowing them to take the test in multiple sessions, either across the school day or in multiple breaks, will allow the student to show what they know. |
| Text to speech software or read aloud | Students who are not reading at grade level are provided with text to speech software or can be read aloud the text. This is only appropriate if the assessment is not related to decoding of text. |
| Speech to text software or scribe | Students who have severe difficulty with writing because of a physical disability or difficulty with spelling can be provided with speech to text software or a scribe who writes a student's response verbatim. This is only appropriate if the test is not measuring spelling or mechanics. |
| Testing modifications | |
| Reduce the amount of questions | Students receive a limited amount of questions rather than taking the whole test. For example, a student is only required to complete 10 out of 20 questions of a test. |
| Provide with questions that are less demanding | Students are provided with only the questions that require less cognitive skills to respond. For example, multiple choice questions with one correct answer. They might be excused from completing an extended response question where they are expected to synthesize across different texts. |
| Test basic skills | Students are provided with a test that only measures basic skills. For example, students are only given questions in which they demonstrate understanding of the standard algorithm for multidigit multiplication. They are excused from extended response questions in which they have to justify their answer. |

guidelines and rules regarding suspensions, which ensure a suspension is not due to a behavior that is a manifestation of their identified disability. Additionally, a student with IEP and behavior problem may require a functional behavior assessment (FBA) and behavior intervention plan (BIP) to ensure their academic and functional success in the school setting (see Figure A.2). It is important to remember that not all students with a disability have behavior problems and not all students with behavior problems will qualify for an IEP.

## Website Resources

### Collaborative for Academic, Social, and Emotional Learning (CASEL)

The CASEL website provides research and resources for evidence-based social emotional learning (SEL) supports. Among the many resources available, CASEL provides a table-rating SEL programs for students in grades PreK-12th grade.
https://casel.org/

| Functional Behavior Assessment (FBA) | • The FBA process uses multiple sources of data to try and zero in on why a student may be displaying a specific undesirable behavior.<br>• A FBA seeks to identify the function of a behavior.<br>• Typically includes observational data collected around A-B-C's (antecedent, behavior, and consequence) of a specific behavior.<br>• A FBA may also include data from student, family, or teacher interviews. |
| --- | --- |
| Behavior Intervention Plan (BIP) | • A BIP is created following a completion of an FBA.<br>• A BIP is typically completed by a multidisciplinary team and tailored to the student's need and interest.<br>• The goal of a BIP is to support the student in understanding appropriate behavioral responses. The plan outlines reinforcements and incentives to promote the student's use of these behaviors.<br>• Specific goals and a plan for progress monitoring should be outlined in the BIP. |

**Figure A.2** Practices for Supporting Students.

*Innovative Resources or Instructional Success (IRIS) Center:*
*Functional Behavior Assessment: Identifying the Reasons*
*for Problem Behavior and Developing a Behavior Plan*

The following module provides an overview of the steps to conducting an FBA and creating a BIP. The estimated completion time for this module is 2 h.
https://iris.peabody.vanderbilt.edu/module/fba/

*Innovative Resources or Instructional Success (IRIS) Center:*
*Addressing the Disruptive and Noncompliant Behaviors*

This two-part module discusses problem behavior, teacher actions, and interventions that can support the decrease of disruptive and noncompliant behaviors. The estimated completion time for both modules is 2 h. Each module takes 1 h to complete.

> **Part 1: Understanding the acting-out cycle**
> https://iris.peabody.vanderbilt.edu/module/bi1/
> **Part 2: Behavioral interventions**
> https://iris.peabody.vanderbilt.edu/module/bi2/

### Print Resources

*Managing Challenging Behaviors in Schools:*
*Research-Based Strategies that Work (What Works*
*for Special-Needs Learners) by Kathleen Lane, Holly*
*Menzies, Allison Bruhn, & Mary Crnobori (2011)*

This text in divided into three parts. In the first part, the authors outline systems to prevent problem behaviors from occurring at the classroom level. In part two, the authors elaborate on several specific practices that educators can use to respond to problem behaviors. The final part of the text discusses how teachers can get started when seeking to address problem behavior in their classroom.

*Supporting Behavior for School Success: A Step-by-*
*Step Guide to Key Strategies by Kathleen Lane, Holly*
*Menzies, Robin Ennis, & Wendy Oakes (2015)*

Each chapter in this text outlines an antecedent management strategy that can be used to support student behavior and reduce the occurrence of undesirable behaviors in the classroom.

## Transition Planning

Transition aids in facilitating a student with disabilities' post-school activities. These post-school activities can include postsecondary education, vocational training, employment, community partnership, continuing adult education, adult services, or independent living. Transition services also include making families and students aware of resources and community partnerships that can support their post-school success. Depending on your state, decisions regarding a student's postsecondary transition' needs are to be discussed and address by the IEP team by the age of 16 (age 14 in some states). Postsecondary goals and services should be outlined within a student's IEP as part of this plan. Additionally, transition planning can include a student's movement from early childhood special education services to K-12 special education services or as a student transitions between school settings.

## *Website Resources*

### *National Technical Assistance Center on Transition (NTACT)*

The National Technical Assistance Center on Transition (NTACT) purpose is to assist in the implementation of evidence-based practices to ensure students with disabilities graduate prepared for employment and postsecondary success. NTACT is funded by the US Department of Education's Office of Special Education Programming and Rehabilitation Services Administration (RSA). https://transitionta.org/

### *Transition of Students with Disabilities to Postsecondary Education: A Guide for High School Educators*

As a part of the US Department of Education's website, this page outlines key components of transition planning as outlined in the Individuals with Disabilities Education Act (IDEA) as well as answers frequently asked questions.
https://www2.ed.gov/about/offices/list/ocr/transitionguide.html

## *Print Resources*

### *Building Alliances: A How-to Manual to Support Transitioning Youth by Valerie L. Mazzotti & Dawn A. Rowe (2015)*

Core principles and practices of collaboration essential for the transition of students with disabilities and their families is detailed in the following text. Additionally, the authors provide several 'research in practice' vignettes and provide a step-by-step approach to promote collaboration among a transition team.

### Transition to Adulthood for Students with Disabilities, Reference Guide by Thomas Gibbon & David Bateman (2018)

The following reference guide is designed to support administrators and educators though the different stages of transition planning as outlined within the Individuals with Disabilities Education Act (IDEA). This guide also outlines relevant federal laws and comes in a laminated trifold format.

### Transition to Adulthood: Work, Community, and Educational Success Edited by L. Lynn Stansberry Brusnahan, Robert A. Stodden, & Stanley H. Zucker (2018)

The following text provides a 'blueprint' for supporting students with disabilities in their postsecondary goals in a variety of settings. This text serves as resource for transition specialist, educators, and administrators through an overview of research and best practice in their area of postsecondary transition practices.

## Bilingual Students and Special Education

Special considerations need to be taken into account when working with students with disabilities who are emergent bilinguals. These considerations include knowing the child's culture of origin, family background, language spoken at home, the child's educational experiences, the child's English language proficiency in the domains of listening, speaking, reading and writing, as well as the child's abilities in their home language. Having these things in mind and using the child's strength will ensure that he or she receives an adequate education.

## Website Resources

### Coloring Colorado

Coloring Colorado provides educators with free evidence-based information and activities to support students who are English learners (ELs) and their families in grades PreK-12. The website contains a variety of helpful articles as well as practical information to help provide ELs with a high-quality education.

https://www.colorincolorado.org/

*Center for Applied Linguistics (CAL)*

CAL is dedicated to providing research, resources, and policy analysis that promotes language learning and cultural understanding. The website contains some free resources as well as paid resources including books and online courses.
http://www.cal.org/

*Innovative Resources or Instructional Success (IRIS)*
*Center: Cultural and Linguistic Differences*

This module helps educators understand the importance of culture and its influence in teaching and learning. The module also provides educators with ways of improving culturally responsive teaching.
https://iris.peabody.vanderbilt.edu/module/clde/

*Innovative Resources or Instructional Success (IRIS) Center:*
*Teaching ELLs*

This module teaches educators about second language acquisition and academic English. This module also provides educators with practical knowledge on how to support English learners through evidence-based instructional practices.
https://iris.peabody.vanderbilt.edu/module/ell/

### Print Resources

*IEPs for ELs: And Other Diverse Learners by*
*John J. Hoover & James R. Patton (2017)*

This book is designed to help educators involved in the special education planning of students who are English learners develop legally defensible plans while keeping language and cultural considerations at the forefront.

### Parents and Families

Family engagement is linked to student achievement. It is important to have multiple opportunities to engage and collaborate with families. The additional needs of students with disabilities require that schools actively seek to engage with families. The unique role of parents and caregivers of students with disabilities has led to the incorporation of 'parent involvement' as one of the six foundational principles of the Individuals with Disabilities Education Act (IDEA).

## *Website Resources*

### *Center for Parent Information and Resources (CPIR)*

CPIR provides schools and other agencies working with families of children with disabilities with evidence-based materials and information on key topics.
https://www.parentcenterhub.org/

### *Understood.org*

Understood.org is a website containing resources, tools, information for parents of children with disabilities. The website contains parent-friendly information regarding the law as it applies for children with disabilities, practical tools that parents can use for a variety of issues facing their children, and tips on how to navigate the special education system.
https://www.understood.org/en/about

## *Print Resources*

### *Parent and Families of Students with Special Needs: Collaborating Across the Age Span by Viki A. McGinley & Melina Alexander (2017)*

This book provides information on how to develop key skills needed to collaborate with parents and families.

## References

Bateman, D. F., & Cline, J. L. (2016). *A teacher's guide to special education.* ASCD.

McLaughlin, M. J., & Nolet, V. (2004). *What every principal needs to know about special education.* Corwin Press.

The Understood Team (n.d.). *IEP terms to know.* Understood. Retrieved November 15, 2019, from https://www.understood.org/en/school-learning/special-services/ieps/iep-terms-to-know

# APPENDIX B

## Implementation Resources

### Edited by Courtney Lynn Barcus

Appendix B is a compilation of the resources that are referenced in each chapter. These resources are intended to support administrators in further building knowledge on each chapter topic, as well as to provide additional external resources that can be used to implement the actions and next steps discussed in each chapter.

Chapter 1: Teacher Preparation
Chapter 2: Teacher Leadership
Chapter 3: Using Data
Chapter 4: Data-Based Individualization
Chapter 5: Instructional Expertise
Chapter 6: Adaptive Expertise
Chapter 7: Collaboration
Chapter 8: Advocacy

### Chapter 1: Teacher Preparation

As school leaders, administrators are responsible for providing the professional growth supports that all educators need to continue their development as professionals. The resources provided here offer clarity on the knowledge and skills that effective special educators must hold, as well as resources to support implementation of effective professional development systems that promote the use of evidence-based practices.

## Website Resources

### Council for Exceptional Children Professional Standards

The Council for Exceptional Children (CEC) is a professional organization for special education professionals, providing resources, professional development, and research for supporting students with exceptional needs. The professional standards linked here have been developed to support clear understanding of the current knowledge and skills that special educators must develop through preparation and professional development.
https://www.cec.sped.org/Standards

### Innovation Configurations

The 'Collaboration for Effective Educator Development, Accountability, and Reform' (CEEDAR) Center's mission is to support the development of effective professional learning structures that will encourage the use of evidence-based practices. The Innovation Configurations were designed to analyze professional learning structures for effective instructional and application practices.
https://ceedar.education.ufl.edu/innovation-configurations/

## Chapter 2: Teacher Leadership

As administrators work to develop special education teacher leadership, Table B.1 provides an example of a completed implementation matrix (Table 2.3) and Figure B.1 provides summaries of schoolwide systems that lend themselves to the leadership skills of the special educator.

## Website Resources

### Center on Positive Behavior Interventions and Supports

This resource is intended to provide information, support, and resources to school leaders seeking to 'establish, scale up, or sustain' The Positive Behavior Interventions and Supports (PBIS) framework. The website is funded by the US Department of Education, Office of Special Education Programing, and Office of Elementary and Secondary Education.
https://www.pbis.org/

**Table B.1** Completed Systematic Inclusive Practices Planning and Implementation Matrix

|  | Academics | Behavior | Interdisciplinary collaboration |
|---|---|---|---|
| **Schoolwide systems** | Harnessing the documentation of MTSS (Multi-Tiered Services and Supports) academic interventions to gather more data to strategically leverage teachers' strengths, monitor student growth, and identify areas where more support is necessary | Creating an interdisciplinary team to focus on addressing the needs of students who exhibit symptoms of depression, anxiety, substance abuse, family issues, trauma, or anger that are beyond the student's control and persist as serious, chronic, or escalated needs despite intervention | Development of Professional Learning Communities that are teacher-led in place of grade-level meetings due to challenges related to scheduling |
| **Instruction** | Transition to a standard district curriculum for the entire school regardless of placement (honors/cotaught/instructional setting), which requires more scaffolding and training for teachers to provide the supports and differentiation needed to teach a curriculum with a higher cognitive demand | Developing and incorporating common language and lessons through advisories for character education, especially to support social emotional learning | Cross-curricular collaboration to help support students' ability to generalize skills across content areas, which encourages students to generalize skills such as argument writing, problem solving, etc. |

(*Continued*)

**Table B.1** Completed Systematic Inclusive Practices Planning and Implementation Matrix (*Continued*)

|  | Academics | Behavior | Interdisciplinary collaboration |
|---|---|---|---|
| **Intervention** | Differentiated supports including tutoring, teacher training, and strategies specific to students who need additional supports as the ELL population grows | Developing a check-in/check-out (CICO) system for students who are frequently removed from class or referred for discipline issues in an effort to improve mediation and reintegration, to prevent problems within the school community | Executive functioning supports that are used universally across content areas for freshmen as they transition to organization in high school with more teachers, independence, and responsibility for academic outcomes |

Positive Behavioral Interventions & Supports (PBIS)

- Schoolwide and classwide framework for supporting *all* students, not just those with disabilities.
- PBIS comprised of a three-tier system where tier one supports are intended for all students school and classroom behaviors.
- Each PBIS tier consists of the following elements: (1) evidence-based practices, (2) stong universal supports with interventions to match student needs, (3) data collection to monitor student progress, and (4) resources to ensure implementation fidelity (Positive Behavioral Interventions and Supports, 2019).

Multi-Tiered Systems of Support (MTSS)

- MTSS, sometimes referred to as Response to Intervention (RTI) combines assessment and intervention to maximize student achievement.
- Data is used to identify students at-risk for poor learning outcomes to assess, plan ongoing progress monitoring, and implement evidence-based interventions.
- Depending on the outcomes of MTSS/RTI a student may be referred to special education, but special education is not the end goal of MTSS/RTI.
- The 4 essential components of MTSS/RTI are: (1) screening, (2) progress monitoring, (3) a multileveled prevention systems, and (4) data-based decision making (American Institutes for Research, 2019).

**Figure B.1** Schoolwide Systems for Special Education Leadership Skills.

## RTI Action Network

The following website outlines seven essential, evidence-based components that contribute to whole system reform and effective implementation of Multi-Tiered Systems of Support (MTSS), PBIS, and response to intervention (RTI). The RTI Action Network is a program of the National Center for Learning Disabilities.

http://www.rtinetwork.org/

## IRIS Learning Modules: RTI

The Innovative Resources for Instructional Success (IRIS) Center, at Vanderbilt University's Peabody College, funded by the US Department of Education's Office of Special Education Programs, is a major resource for evidence-based practices for all educators. The links below connect to a series of learning modules aimed at outlining the MTSS/RTI process, with an emphasis on how to build support for MTSS/RTI, as well as additional considerations for schoolwide implementation.

> **Part 1:** An Overview; https://www.iris.peabody.vanderbilt.edu/module/rti01/
>
> **Part 2:** Assessment; https://iris.peabody.vanderbilt.edu/module/rti02/
>
> **Part 3:** Reading Instruction; https://www.iris.peabody.vanderbilt.edu/module/rti03/
>
> **Part 4:** Putting it all Together; https://www.iris.peabody.vanderbilt.edu/module/rti04/
>
> **Part 5:** A Closer Look at Tier 3; https://www.iris.peabody.vanderbilt.edu/module/rti05/
>
> **MTSS/RTI** Mathematics; https://www.iris.peabody.vanderbilt.edu/module/rti-math/
>
> **Considerations for School Leaders**; https://www.iris.peabody.vanderbilt.edu/module/rti-leaders/

## Print Resources

*Class-wide Positive Behavior Interventions and Supports:*
*A Guide to Proactive Classroom Management*
*by Brandi Simonsen & Diane Myers (2014)*

The following text outlines the three respective tiers of implementing PBIS at the classroom level. The text contains vignettes and resources to support teacher's classroom management and intervention implementation.

*The PBIS Team Handbook: Setting Expectations*
*and Building Positive Behavior by Char Ryan*
*& Beth Baker (2019)*

This user-friendly guide is designed to support teams, coaches, and administrators in the implementation of PBIS. Tips, visuals, and a free downloadable study guide are available.

## Chapter 3: Using Data

The links provided are intended to support schools to use data to drive improvement. Administrators will find resources for data collection, interventions for schoolwide growth, as well as staff supports.

## Website Resources

*Data Quality Campaign: Why Education Data?*

The Data Quality Campaign is a nonprofit organization with the goal of ensuring all members of the education community have a high understanding and access to data that can be used to make effective educational decisions. This website provides tools and resources for data-driven school improvement that can support all stakeholder groups.
https://dataqualitycampaign.org/why-education-data/

*10 Data Tracking Apps You Can Use in Your Class Tomorrow*

This link, from Georgia Public Broadcasting (GPA) a state network of Public Broadcast Service (PBS) and National Public Radio (NPR), details a variety of tablet and cell phone applications that can be used at the classroom level for academic and behavioral data collection.
http://www.gpb.org/blogs/education-matters/2016/12/13/10-data-tracking-apps-you-can-use-your-class-tomorrow

*Data Basic #1: Knowledge of Data Collection Tools*

The University of Nebraska-Lincoln, supported by the Nebraska Department of Education, has developed 'The Student Engagement Project' to support individualized student planning. This link includes a number of data collection tools, implementation plans, and printable guides.
https://k12engagement.unl.edu/databasic1#Q1

*An LEA or School Guide for Identifying Evidence-*
*Based Interventions for School Improvement*

The Florida Center for Reading Research provides resources related to evidence-based interventions for school improvement through the evaluation, identification, and implementation of interventions.
http://fcrr.org/documents/essa/essa_guide_lea.pdf

*How School District Leaders Can Support the Use*
*of Data to Improve Teaching and Learning*

This policy brief from ACT Research and Policy provides information on the use of data to improve school practices.
http://www.act.org/content/dam/act/unsecured/documents/Use-of-Data.pdf

*Administrator Goals: Guidance, Exemplars,*
*and Optional Goal-Setting Template*

The State of New Jersey's Department of Education provides this training specifically for administrators on writing SMART goals aimed at school-wide improvement.
https://www.state.nj.us/education/AchieveNJ/teacher/iqt/training/AdministratorGoals.pdf

## Chapter 4: Data-Based Individualization

To ensure a smooth roll out of DBI, all staff members involved must be well informed on its various components. With the help of the special educator, carefully planned professional development and coaching should be implemented. Listed below are resources to support the development of these structures.

### Website Resources

*The National Center on Intensive Intervention (NCII)*

NCII provides stakeholders with information and resources that support the implementation of intensive intervention in reading, math, and behavior for students with severe and persistent learning and/or behavior needs. Examples of evidence-based interventions and modules on the DBI process are available.
https://intensiveintervention.org/

## What Works Clearinghouse (WWC)

WWC, a development of the Institute of Education Sciences (IES) within the US Department of Education, provides administrators with the latest evidence of effectiveness on various interventions, products, and practices. https://ies.ed.gov/ncee/wwc/

## IRIS Modules

The two-part module series provides in-depth information on data-based individualization. Participants learn the process of adapting and intensifying interventions based on student level data.

> **Part 1:** Using Data-Based Individualization to Intensify Instruction
> https://iris.peabody.vanderbilt.edu/module/dbi1/
> **Part 2:** Collecting and Analyzing Data for Data-Based Individualization
> https://iris.peabody.vanderbilt.edu/module/dbi2/

## Chapter 5: Instructional Expertise

Special educators showcase their instructional expertise through their extensive pedagogical knowledge, expertise in learning, and their focus on vertical planning all applied with an individual student view. They utilize various tools to engage in these processes. Resources below include instructional strategy support, planning resources for vertical alignment, and a variety of assessment tools.

## Website Resources

### The UDL Guidelines

The Universal Design for Learning (UDL) is a framework for teaching and learning, based on research in the field of neuroscience, which addresses the strengths and needs of all students and provides a variety of ways to engage with content, access material, and show learning. These guidelines can be used by administrators and educators to support all learners. http://udlguidelines.cast.org/

### Achieve the Core

Special educators explicitly plan for vertical alignment to address the wide range of needs and abilities in a classroom. Achievethecore.org provides ample resources for developing both literacy and mathematics standards-aligned instruction that can be vertically tracked in order to effectively differentiate instruction. In addition, a lesson planning tool is available and videos of standards aligned instruction can be viewed.

### Leadership resources:

• Administrators and instructional coaches can use the 'Instructional Practices Guides' to provide content-based feedback to teachers. The guides provide observation documentation resources and probing questions that can be used with teachers when debriefing the lesson.

### Literacy resources:

• Instructional content resources are available for breaking down 'text complexity', 'text-dependent questions', and 'foundational skills'.

### Mathematics resources:

• 'Where to Focus' grade-level maps and K-8 progression guides help educators identify the major works at each grade level.
• The 'Coherence Map' shows how each standard and substandard connects to those above, below, and within the grade level.

https://achievethecore.org

*Interest Inventory*

Interest inventories can be used to learn more about student interests and motivation. This site links to a list of questions that can be used to get to know individual students.
https://education.msu.edu/research/projects/eteams/pdf_s/VALUE_StudentInterestInventory.pdf

### Print Resources

*Universal Design for Learning: Theory and Practice*
*by Anne Meyer, David H. Rose, & David Gordon*

This text provides a comprehensive overview of the UDL Framework including the history and evolution of UDL, details on learner variability, guidelines for implementation, and practical advice.

The interactive text is also available at http://udltheorypractice.cast.org/login

## Chapter 6: Adaptive Expertise

Professional Learning Communities (PLCs) are impactful spaces for the adaptive expertise of special educators to be turned from the classroom environment toward whole-school orientations. These resources provide concrete steps for implementing PLCs.

### *Website Resources*

#### *Planning Professional Learning from Professional Learning: Reimagined Published by Educational Leadership*

This quick read discusses supporting and implementing Professional Learning Communities and ideas for evaluating professional learning. This evaluation can be helpful in determining where to assign adaptive experts. http://www.ascd.org/publications/educational-leadership/may14/vol71/num08/Planning-Professional-Learning.aspx

#### *Professional Learning Communities: School Leaders' Perspectives*

Adaptive experts often possess social and professional capital, which can be applied within PLCs. This case-study-specific piece includes important starting points and supports for beginning or reconstituting the PLC process. http://www.ascd.org/publications/newsletters/education-update/aug08/vol50/num08/Professional-Learning-Communities@-School-Leaders'-Perspectives.aspx

#### *Best Practices for Professional Learning Communities*

This article discusses six steps that are typically taken within the PLC process. Administrators and teams can utilize the clear steps and supporting documentation to implement systems for effective PLCs. Links to additional resources are also available. https://www.educationworld.com/a_admin/best-practices-for-professional-learning-communities.shtml

#### *The Power of Professional Capital*

Professional capital plays an important role for special educators and other adaptive experts. This adapted keynote address identifies how the career stage of an educator affects their professional capital and the implications therein. http://www.michaelfullan.ca/wp-content/uploads/2013/08/JSD-Power-of-Professional-Capital.pdf

## Chapter 7: Collaboration

Resources here will assist administrators in establishing strong, effective, and schoolwide collaboration. Resources are provided for supporting collaboration within the school, for establishing effective co-teaching practices, and for integrating parents and community in collaborative efforts.

## *Website Resources*

### *IRIS Learning Module Effective School Practices: Promoting Collaboration and Monitoring Students' Academic Achievement*

This IRIS module provides information regarding partnerships between general education and special education staff. It highlights the importance of collaboration in setting high expectations for all students through collective responsibility.
https://iris.peabody.vanderbilt.edu/module/esp/

### *Swift Guide – Family and Community Engagement Resources*

The Swift Education Center includes resources on family and community engagement that assist in the creation of a collaborative school culture. Both the family and community pages include short videos highlighting the key factors for collaboration, as well as viewing guides to support school teams in processing the content. Print resources contain action steps to continue the process.
http://guide.swiftschools.org/family-community-engagement/trusting-family-partnerships
http://guide.swiftschools.org/family-community-engagement/trusting-community-partnerships

## *Print Resources*

### *Co-Teaching: Making It Work by Educational Leadership, December 2015/January 2016, 73(4)*

This issue of **Educational Leadership** includes several practical articles to support schools in considering various topics related to co-teaching.
*The issue can be purchased and many free articles are available at* http://www.ascd.org/publications/educational-leadership/dec15/vol73/num04/toc.aspx

## Chapter 8: Advocacy

Advocacy comes in many forms and requires specific skills and competencies. The resources provided here will support administrators and educators as they build the skills and competencies necessary for effective advocacy.

## *Website Resources*

### *The Arc*

The Arc is a national community-based organization which focuses on advocacy for and with people who have intellectual and developmental disabilities. These useful links offer information on services, supports, and events. https://thearc.org/

### *Council for Exceptional Children: Policy & Advocacy*

CEC provides information on policy, advocacy, and legislative information. Parents and educators alike may find these resources useful. https://www.cec.sped.org/Policy-and-Advocacy

### *Learning Disabilities Association of America (LDA): Disability Rights and Advocacy*

LDA is an association of parents and professionals advocating for the rights of students with learning disabilities. This page provides a collection of links offering information for parents, educators, and professionals on advocacy, disability rights, and legal issues. https://ldaamerica.org/advocacy/disability-rights-and-advocacy/

### *Parent Advocacy Coalition for Educational Rights (PACER)*

The PACER center, funded by the US Department of Education's Office of Special Education Programs, offers ample resources including information on IEP and 504 plans, transition supports, dispute resolution, mental health supports, and much more. In addition, events, workshops, and youth groups are offered. http://www.pacer.org

## References

American Institutes for Research. (n.d.). *Essential components of RTI*. Center on Response to Intervention. https://rti4success.org/essential-components-rti

Center on Positive Behavioral Interventions and Supports (PBIS). (n.d.). *Tiered framework*. https://www.pbis.org/pbis/tiered-framework

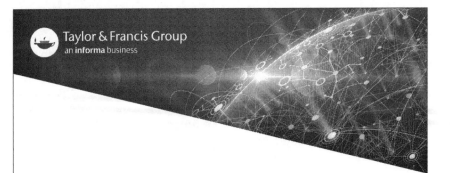